C0-AWT-179

Set No Limits

Set No Limits

A Rebuttal to Daniel Callahan's Proposal to Limit Health Care for the Elderly

EDITED BY

Robert L. Barry, O.P., and Gerard V. Bradley

PROLOGUE BY

Nat Hentoff

UNIVERSITY OF ILLINOIS PRESS
Urbana and Chicago

© 1991 by the Board of Trustees of the University of Illinois
Manufactured in the United States of America
C   5   4   3   2   1

This book is printed on acid-free paper.

Library of Congress Cataloging-in-Publication Data

Set no limits: a rebuttal to Daniel Callahan's proposal to limit
   health care for the elderly / edited by Robert L. Barry and Gerard
   V. Bradley; prologue by Nat Hentoff.
        p.   cm.
   Includes bibliographical references.
   ISBN 0-252-01860-5
   1. Aged—Medical care—Moral and ethical aspects. 2. Right to
die. 3. Callahan, Daniel, 1930– Setting limits. I. Barry,
Robert Laurence. II. Bradley, Gerard V., 1954– .
RA564.8.S465 1991
362.1'9897'001—dc20   91-10448
                                                                     CIP

Contents

Preface

Life. Whether the "highest" of a hierarchically ordered set of several basic goods, the common morality of Western societies has traditionally held it immune from direct attack. "One may never intentionally destroy an innocent human life" was the formulation. There was never any question of the utter destruction of the entire human being. The Western philosophical and moral tradition generally has defined death as the separation of body and soul, and as long as orthodox Christianity established the fundamental values of Western culture, the belief was maintained that the physical body would in some way be restored to life at the end of time.

In Western Christian culture, another lesson was quite clear: physical, bodily existence was a basic good to be respected. This meant that killing could not be tolerated except in the most extreme conditions. Innocent human beings were never to be deliberately killed by either public authorities or private citizens. Only those known to have committed acts worthy of death were allowed to be deliberately killed by private citizens. Even when killing was justified and martyrdom honored, the intention could never be to destroy life.

In this tradition, life was a good; death—its negation—was an evil. So tradition. But tradition did not include genetic engineering, ventilators, artificial lungs, dialysis, or organ transplants. Tradition originated before modern scientific medicine made it possible to postpone death for those who were dying, before artificial nutrition and hydration could keep the comatose, who were not dying, alive for decades. The fundamental question at this juncture is on the table, up for grabs: *is* life a good, and death an evil? Always? Sometimes? For some persons and not for others? In some value systems but not in others? Upon what basis can a socially authoritative answer be founded? It would appear that traditional Western morality has lost its dominance over ways of thinking about life and death.

These questions will not go away. Two profound challenges to our powers of moral and political deliberation will not let them: one, the burgeoning movement for a "right-to-die," and, second, issues surrounding medical care and treatment for the elderly. The most recent episodes are the U.S. Supreme Court's June 1990 decision in the Nancy Cruzan case, in which the Court did not allow assisted feeding and hydration to be removed from seriously brain-damaged patients without clear and convincing evidence that the patient desired this, and Daniel Callahan's provocative book *Setting Limits*. In the *Cruzan* case, the Court held that individuals have a "liberty interest" in rejecting medical treatments, including assisted feeding, even though many would consider such an action suicidal. However, it held that such a decision could not be made by others and that it would be constitutionally appropriate for states to limit the authority of proxy decision-makers to withdraw or withhold medical treatment. In his book Callahan argued that after one has lived out a reasonable life span of seventy-five or so years, society ought not permit valuable medical resources to be devoted to prevent one's demise. Each movement inescapably raises fundamental questions.

A conference held at the University of Illinois College of Law in October 1989 explored these issues. This volume, which contains the fruits of that effort, offers a critical approach to Callahan's proposal. Lest it be thought that we are merely "ganging up" on Callahan, it should be recalled that the Hastings Center, of which Callahan is the cofounder and director, has had a close relationship with the American Medical Association (AMA) for years. As a result of this relationship, the ethical positions adopted by the Hastings Center and promoted by Callahan have usually become those adopted by the AMA. For example, the moral positions espoused by the Hastings Center on abortion, care of handicapped infants, and withdrawal of assisted feeding soon became those officially approved of by the AMA. Thus, in raising questions about Callahan's proposal, questions are being raised about a policy that might well be adopted by one of the most influential lobbying organizations in the nation. Rather than "ganging up" on an ivory tower academic, the authors of the essays herein are challenging a position that may well be imposed on this nation by a wealthy and extremely powerful profession.

Nat Hentoff's keynote remarks on the "Indivisibility of Life" provide an appropriate prologue to the volume. The two essays in Part One explore the moral foundations of (most particularly) Callahan's manifesto. Robert Barry, a principal organizer of the conference, has added to his essay, "Mandatory, Universal Age-Based Rationing of Scarce Medical Resources," and argues that Callahan's proposal is an example of "medical totalitarianism" and is contrary to justice because it imposes far greater burdens on the elderly than it does on any other age category. Robert George argues that Callahan's proposal "inverts" the Western moral and legal tradition: now, death is or can be a good; life is or can be an evil.

In Part Two Hadley Arkes examines the moral underpinnings of the right-to-die and includes critical comment on the U.S. Supreme Court decision in the Nancy Cruzan case. Arkes concludes that right-to-die arguments are characteristically incoherent: they amount to confessions of, in his felicitous phrase, "a right to do a wrong." He shows that the inverted logic of Callahan's claims opens the door to the highly skewed logic of the right-to-die. Callahan's myopic view and the twisted logic of his age-based rationing system have led us to the contorted logic of *Cruzan,* and we can expect even further skewing of normal logic because of Callahan's views. Arkes's assertions are relevant to the issues discussed in Callahan's book because Callahan claims that doing a wrong to the elderly (denying them even minimally expensive life-preserving treatment) to preserve the financial integrity of life is permissible in contemporary circumstances.

Robert Destro's essay locates the philosophical ground for such claims in prevailing conceptions of individual autonomy, and it criticizes Callahan's proposal as discriminatory against the elderly. He has probably located the cornerstone of the new morality that supports, even produces, a right-to-die movement and that helps explain the plausibility of Callahan's recommendations.

In Part Three, which concludes the volume, Marshall Kapp and Lawrence DeBrock each bring the discussion to a more policy-oriented focus. Kapp effectively dissects Callahan's proposal from the perspective of constitutional law and public health, and DeBrock, an academic economist, addresses one critical prop of Callahan's proposal, the coming (relative) scarcity of medical resources. DeBrock persuasively questions such predictions and tellingly replies that the economics of health care in even the intermediate future are too uncertain to support a present decision to ration.

We wish to thank the many contributors to this conference. Dr. Morton Weir, chancellor of the University of Illinois, contributed heavily, as did Bishop John Myers, Roman Catholic bishop of Peoria, and Msgr. Edward Duncan, director of the Newman Foundation at the University of Illinois. The College of Law not only provided facilities for the conference but also contributed generously. We thank Richard Wentworth of University of Illinois Press for his enthusiastic support for the work and for his expert guidance in bringing this book to publication, and Susan Patterson and Terry Sears for their editorial expertise.

Robert L. Barry, O.P.
Gerard V. Bradley

Prologue
The Indivisibility of Life

NAT HENTOFF

Crassly put: Are the elderly worth it? . . . The growing ranks of
the elderly are putting pressure on government to assume more
and more of their costs. But in an era where budget deficits are
the overriding problem, where will the money come from? . . .

With 28% of Medicare's budget going to patients in their last
year, are Americans paying merely to extend life without making
it more worth living? Will the U.S. ultimately have to ration
health care and deny it to the very old?
                                    —Lee Smith, *Fortune,* March 29, 1989

First, some cautionary riffs, to adapt a term used by elderly jazz musicians.

The first is by Justice Louis Brandeis: "The greatest dangers to liberty
[and I would add, to life] lurk in insidious encroachment by men of
zeal—well-meaning but without understanding."

The second I heard from a woman in Pennsylvania who told me it is an
ancient folk saying—a survival saying: "Once you put a price tag on life,
inevitably it will be marked down." I would paraphrase that to: "Once you
put an *age* limit on life, inevitably it will be marked down."

And finally a columnist in a weekly newspaper, *Catholic New York*—one of
the advantages of being an atheist is you can quote from any religious source
without being accused of proselytizing for religion. The columnist is Father
James Gilhooley: "An afternoon spent at Dachau a quarter of a century ago
taught me to beware of all those who would improve life by first destroying it."

The utilitarian idea of rationing certain kinds of health care—and therefore,
ineluctably, life itself—did not originate with Daniel Callahan.

In 1983, reading an article in the *Yale Law Journal,* "A Structural Analysis
of the Physician-Patient Relationship in No-Code Decisionmaking," I came
across a footnote with much more evocative language than the title: A
physician was "less likely to resuscitate the aged because *the physician equated
advanced age with a decline in social capacity*" (emphasis added). That was one
source of information. The author also stated: "The aged are more frequently

pronounced dead after a cursory examination. . . . and alcoholics, prosti-
tutes, drug addicts and vagrants received less active resuscitation efforts."

The elderly, you see, are not exclusively subject to this kind of terminal
bias. They have equally useless companions. In the June 1984 edition of
the *Journal of Public Health,* the dean of the University of Vermont College
of Medicine, in speaking of the need to bring health costs down, noted that
"further emphasis on preventive medicine would result in more persons
living longer, increasing the financial drain by the elderly on the working
population." Mind you, the reference here is to *preventive* medicine, not to
the specter that Callahan invokes: expensive, high-technology life-extending
medicine.

The targeted elderly—at least those who want to contribute to the public
good and not just think of themselves—would apparently be best advised to
follow the advice of former Governor Richard Lamm of Colorado: step
aside. Dylan Thomas, an incurable individualist, is to be ignored. Do go
gently into that good night. And be sure to go.

But then again, given the nature of human nature, there will always
be sizeable numbers of people who have to be slid or pushed into
that good night. Or, as Callahan puts it in his book, *What Kind of Life?:*
if it is necessary to control health costs, and one is serious about that,
then the clear historical record shows that it is naive to believe it can
be done wholly by self-restraint on the part of individuals and private
institutions.

The government, then, must save us from allegedly disastrous health
costs by giving the elderly—at least those without resources except for
Medicare—no choice but to die earlier *in the public interest.*

Who will decide? First, Congress will decide. And then, implementing
the customary shadowy will of Congress, will be the kind of apparatchiks
who now serve you at the windows of the Department of Motor Vehicles.

Callahan often refers to this design for the future as a "new vision" of
health care. It is, of course, not so new. Those on welfare and the working
poor have had long experience with the realities of that vision. Limits have
been set for them all their lives. And the elderly were experiencing limits
well before the 1987 publication of Callahan book's *Setting Limits,* which
tried—and has, to some extent, succeeded—in legitimizing what has not
before been said where the laity could hear.

In 1986 Dr. Norman Levinsky, chief of medicine at Boston University
Medical Center—and proof that not all bioethicists are members of a new
priesthood of death—told me: "I have no question that some physicians
and other caregivers consider the life of someone over 80 to be less worthy
than that of someone who is 28." A year before, Dr. Levinsky had written in
the Boston *Globe:*

I can agree with the abstract principle that intensive methods should not be used merely to extend the process of dying. The problem comes when I try to apply it to individual patients. Let me describe a specific case:

Last year an 88-year-old woman was brought to our emergency floor, suffering from sudden failure of breathing and reduction in blood pressure.

Our doctors felt initially that she was "as good as dead" but tried to resuscitate her. A tube was put down her throat and connected to a machine which breathed for her. Her blood pressure was raised by medication infused through another tube into one of her veins. She was transferred to the intensive care unit, where vigorous treatment continued. Over the next few weeks the patient recovered completely. She returned home and since then has been living self-sufficiently, enjoying the company of her children and grandchildren nearby.

The lifespan of mankind may be three-score years and ten, as the Psalmist wrote, but the lifespan of an individual man or woman is not known until he or she dies. A decision to discontinue life-sustaining treatment leads to a self-fulfilling prophecy about that patient's natural time to die....

Our society places unique value in the life of each individual. Doctors who fight for life exalt that principle in practice. It is not death with dignity to die before one's time.

But *does* our society place unique value on the life of each individual? Callahan is hardly the only advocate of reducing health costs who believes that the elderly past a certain age—somewhere in the eighties, let us say—ought *not* to be reimbursed by the government for treatment in any intensive care unit unless there are "high probabilities of good outcome." So much for the eighty-eight-year-old woman on Dr. Levinsky's emergency floor, whom doctors there considered "as good as dead."

The *individual* and his or her needs are an increasing obstacle to efficiency in our society—and not only cost-efficiency. Individual privacy, for example, greatly concerned the framers of the Constitution. And that's why we have the Fourth Amendment—or what's left of it—written in the most specific terms of any element in the Bill of Rights. But under the Burger and now the Rehnquist Court, the Fourth Amendment has been continually eroded on behalf of enabling police and court procedures to be less impeded by individual rights. Without, I expect, having thought about it all, those who would ration health care for the elderly are very much a part of this diminishing of *individual* rights and liberties.

Consider, for instance, the debate on individual differences among the elderly. Dr. Edward Schneider at the University of California, Los Angeles, has noted in the *Journal of the American Medical Association* (February 10, 1989): "When age is employed as a criterion for decision-making, it infers that older individuals make up a homogeneous group. [However], every health practitioner is aware of the enormous heterogeneity in the process

of aging. . . .with some individuals having significant declines in functions
. . . .while others have minimal impairment."

On the other hand, there is the answer of those who believe it essential
to consider the elderly as a group, rather than one by one, if limits of life
are to be set for them. As Callahan put it in a 1989 Washington, D.C.,
conference under the auspices of the National Legal Center for the Medically
Dependent and the Disabled:

> But is it not the case that the elderly are quite varied, that in fact they may
> have far greater differences in their health status at a given chronological age
> than any other age group? That is perfectly true, but it is a mistake to
> conclude from that fact that we must therefore tailor elderly entitlement
> programs to those individual differences.
>
> If it is the case . . . that we cannot possibly meet all individual curative
> needs on the frontier of aging—that is inherently impossible—then we should
> not base policy on the premise that we can. Nor should we base policy on the
> no less true fact that individual people have different life goals and aspirations.
> That is, because some people might like, for example, to live to 100 or 105,
> and might require enormous resources to make that possible, that should be
> their right under public entitlement programs.

Or presumably, if Callahan's cut-off age for Medicare benefits for certain
life-sustaining treatment turns out to be eighty-seven, the individual who
wants to live longer, if he or she can, may have to die sooner under
collective cost-efficiency norms.

Callahan continues:

> This is only to say that we can no longer afford a highly individualistic
> policy if, at the same time, we insist upon the unlimited pursuit of technologi-
> cal progress to meet individual needs. We should instead begin devising policy
> with some more general view of the common good of all age groups in view.
>
> In the provision of health care to the elderly, my approach would be to
> see if we could achieve a public consensus on what counts as a reasonable
> level of health care for the elderly and reasonable limits on that care. Instead
> of working with individual needs and interests, I propose we work with
> the idea of trying to help the elderly *as a group* avoid a premature death
> and achieve a *decently* long, full life span (emphasis added).
>
> While individual elderly people may want more, and could even benefit
> from more, we will have done our duty to them in our public entitlement
> programs if we could get them through a full life span, *by which I mean
> the late 70's or early 80's.* We should simultaneously work to greatly improve
> long-term and home care for the frail elderly, and make a variety of other
> needed changes to improve the daily life of the elderly (emphasis added). . . .
>
> Compared with the present Medicare program, some individuals might suffer
> and be worse off—those who might benefit from some future technological
> benefit that might extend their lives into the late 80's or 90's. But I am

convinced *the elderly as a group* would be better off, as would other age groups as well (emphasis added).

This prescription by Callahan, then, is a further dent in Levinsky's notion that our society places a unique value on the life of each of us. On the other hand, although much respectful attention has been paid by some bio-ethicists and caregivers to Callahan's modest proposal for limiting the life-spans of the elderly, there has been opposition.

One of the most vivid dissenters was a woman who stood during the question period after Callahan and I had engaged in a debate before a large audience at an annual conference of the National Counsel on the Aging. Her question was for Callahan. She looked to be in her seventies, and I found out later that she runs a multiple service center for the elderly in Alaska. "Dr. Callahan," she said, "are you aware that you are advocating female genocide?" He was stunned. She helped him out. "Women live longer than men," she pointed out. Far more women than men would be deprived of life-sustaining treatment under the Callahan vision.

Other objections have concerned the constitutionality of the Callahan plan. As a clubhouse lawyer, it occurred to me that this plan to foreshorten the lives of people on the basis of age and class—class coming into play because the elderly who can afford to do without Medicare will live longer—was in contempt of the Fourteenth Amendment, which says: "No State shall deny to any person within its jurisdiction the equal protection of the laws." To say that because you are past a certain age and of meager financial resources, you are not entitled to have your life sustained, puts you on a decidedly unequal footing with those fortunate enough to be younger. I brought this analysis to Norman Dorsen, professor of law at New York University and president of the American Civil Liberties Union. Dorsen agreed. The concept, he said, was indeed in violation of the equal protection clause of the Fourteenth Amendment.

Callahan and others of his persuasion disagree. Callahan says: "The Medicare program itself, requiring that one be 65 to participate, is already an age-based program, the only one for any age group in this country.... A limitation on that program, using age as a standard, should no more run afoul of the Constitution than the age bias of the program itself."

It is one thing to confer health care benefits on the basis of age—as in programs benefitting women and children below the poverty line. But it is a quite different matter to *deprive* people of life-sustaining care *solely* on the basis of their age. What right is more fundamental than staying alive—unless a compelling state interest can be shown to justify govern-mental decisions that would result in the ending of that life? And where would that compelling state interest be found in the Constitution?

But who knows? It could happen. Consider, then, the values that will flow from a societal decision that a compelling state interest in cutting costs justifies cutting off lives. That's not a slippery slope. That's an abyss. Apart from the Constitution, Callahan himself focused on the fundamental unfairness of his plan during an exchange on the December 25, 1988, "MacNeil/Lehrer News Hour." He said that after the fluctuating magical age of termination—which at the time he thought was eighty or eighty-five—"injustice might set in." However, he added, "it seems to me in the nature of the case, it [the injustice] would not be for a very long time."

But why not? Because those being treated unjustly would soon be dead. "It's a kind of trade-off," he said. For the greater good of the society. There are certain historical echoes here. But there are other, less collectively lethal visions. Dr. Edward Schneider, a gerontologist, proposes increasing "biomedical research into the disorders that afflict older persons": Alzheimer's disease, Parkinson's disease, osteoarthritis, osteoporosis, for instance. Each of them "increases exponentially with aging." Each produces "years of disability that require expensive long-term health care." But—using Alzheimer's disease as a measure—research funding "amounts to 0.1 to 0.2 percent of the cost of services to the victim."

That's one alternative to setting terminal limits. But it is also useful to examine—to paraphrase the title of Callahan's new book—what kind of society we want? Dr. Robert Binstock of Case Western University School of Medicine said in March 1989 at the annual meeting of the Gerontological Society of America that even if the percentage of the gross national product (GNP) devoted to health care were to climb to 15 percent, that would hardly destroy the nation. Much more damaging to society, he noted, "would be the age divisiveness and decadent moral climate created by a governmental policy that officially denies life-extending health care because of a person's age."

Callahan, however, foresees a lyrical community of mutual caring and respect as twilight deepens if his modest proposal were to take effect. Instead, of course, there would be warfare among the generations—much more bitter than is already being predicted. Do not expect the aged to welcome the dying of the light, no matter what Callahan and Congress do. Indeed, listen to Belle Rothberg in a September 7, 1989, letter to the New York *Times*. She was responding to a previous letter that advised "fellow oldsters to die with dignity" and "go gentle into that good night." Wrote Belle Rothberg:

> The letter writer believes we "soak up an unfair share of the health budget." . . .
> What it's about [is] money. It's not care for the elderly, not the contributions

they make, not the spirit of these same elderly, who marched on picket lines and in demonstrations and lent their vitality and intelligence to work in public and private institutions to make possible those benefits the "young" do not disdain to accept: Social Security, unemployment insurance, fair wages, among others.

Now they would deny *us* those benefits. Well, we're not going to let them. We're not going to lie down and die. We will do exactly what Dylan Thomas advises, "Rage, rage, against the dying of the light," which they are so eager to darken for us. . . . As for dying with dignity, dying is not a dignified act.

At the 1989 meeting of the Gerontological Society of America, Dr. Christine Cassel, professor of medicine and director of geriatrics at the University of Chicago Pritzker School of Medicine, made several points that ought to be circulated to the populace at large, for they—the electorate—will ultimately determine the question of rationing life by age. As reported on *Family Practice News*, Dr. Cassel said: "What would be so terrible about spending 15% or more of the GNP on health care? Let me remind you that money doesn't just go into a big black hole. It pays people's salaries. It develops new products that can be bought and sold on the open market. It stimulates the economy." She also noted that "government-sanctioned, age-based rationing would 'let doctors off the hook' and spare them from the difficult decisions they ought properly to be making on a case-by-case basis together with elderly patients and their families. I don't trust doctors to implement rationing. My argument is: don't make it any easier for harried physicians to get through a busy day by short-shifting difficult patients."

And Cassel emphasized that age-based, health-care rationing would destroy public trust in physicians: the trust of elderly patients and those who will become elderly. "There are more than 5 million Americans over age 85," said Cassel. "That's a lot of people to let die in any arbitrary or automatic fashion. That has to have a huge impact on the moral fiber of society."

Furthermore, as the Atlanta *Constitution* observed in an editorial on age-based rationing of health care: "What if the cost savings Daniel Callahan envisions fail to materialize? Who would be sacrificed then? 70-year-olds? The disabled? Others beside Dr. Cassel are apprehensive about what will happen to the moral fiber of society if the Callahan way of prioritizing becomes law. They have some reason to be worried. In September, 1989, the first National Conference of the State Judiciary on Bioethical Issues was held—perhaps appropriately—in Reno. Counseling the judges were various bioethicists. Bioethicists, like cremation, is indeed a growth industry.

One of those present, Iowa District Court Judge George Stigler sounded like an apostle of Callahan: "In 1989, there were more people over 65 than there were under 18. 'For every two people working by the time I turn 65, one person will be drawing Social Security.' So, he said, considering the money needed to take care of pregnant women and drug-addicted children, 'economics being economics, the older people may have to do without. . . .With only X amount of money going around, you can't afford to waste it.' "

That is, waste it on the elderly.

In debates and on the telephone, Callahan has told me that he is practically alone in his vision of the future. He tells of the invective he receives, the lack of understanding. But, in fact, he has more admirers than he acknowledges: among physicians, among bioethicists, among more and more judges who do not want to have to deal in their courts with such thorny problems as the removing of feeding tubes and respirators. If the elderly never get to that stage, life would be easier for their relatives, for judges—and, they all say, for the departed souls themselves.

I do not know how many legislators find age-based rationing of life appealing. My guess is that whatever they may feel personally, they fear the political power of the elderly. Some of the aged, as Callahan takes pride in acknowledging, support his plan. But many more do not.

Whatever political judgments are made in the years ahead will largely depend on whether enough of the elderly can be convinced that they are—in former Governor Lamm's gracious phrase—"in the way." That they will be a burden on their families, on the children of the poor, on society as a whole—if they insist on being greedy for more and more life. (That really is what Callahan is talking about: undeserved greed for life.)

Most of the television films on this and allied subjects, like euthanasia, make going gently into the good night a painless, glowing act of transcendence. The departing soul vanishes into the mist to the strains of Woody Guthrie's "So Long, It's Been Good to Know You," played by a string quartet. And most of the feature stories in newspapers also pay tribute to those old folks who know when it is time to go.

The media would be outraged if told they were popularizing the Third Reich concept of "useless eaters," but they have wholly accepted the doctrine that life has to be judged by its *quality* and increasingly by its age. If that quality is found wanting, that life must be marked down until it has lost so much value that it must be removed from the selling floor.

As of now, a bill to ration health care by age alone would not make it out of committee in Congress. But its time may well come unless those of us who see what this will do to the quality of *our* lives—let alone the immediate societal discards—get involved in the debate. And not only in professional journals.

Saul Alinsky used to say that if you don't get into the arena—the public arena—on certain matters, you'll have lost a chance to make a difference—a real difference in people's lives—including how long they are to live. This is surely one of those matters. A matter of thumbs up or thumbs down to millions of Americans, and ultimately, of course, to each of us.

PART ONE

---

*Moral and Ethical Aspects of
Age-Based Rationing*

1

Mandatory, Universal Age-Based Rationing of Scarce Medical Resources

ROBERT L. BARRY, O.P.

In early 1987 the renowned medical ethicist Daniel Callahan argued in *Setting Limits* that radical measures were necessary to assure the future security of the American health care system.[1] Because of an increasing number of elderly and medically dependent persons, and a rapidly decreasing number of younger Americans, Callahan concluded that the system's economic soundness is threatened. For Callahan, it is a demographic certainty that radical measures would have to be taken to protect the health care system.

But what radical measures? Callahan argued that a just and fair system of allocating scarce health care resources would allow denial of nursing care or medical treatments to all elderly persons after they reached the end of their "natural life-span," which could be anywhere from the early seventies to the mid-eighties. To assure equity and prevent unequal distribution of burdens he would require all those living beyond their natural lifespan to participate in the program and allow them to receive *only* pain relief in the event of illness.[2] Only if this system is compulsory and all-encompassing would it effectively curb spending for medical resources, for if any exceptions were to be accepted in principle, the entire system would collapse.

Though Callahan considers denying care only to those elderly persons who consume many resources, he eventually rejects this option and accepts the negative consequences of a universal and mandatory system of rationing.

Would we not, however, have bought those developments at a high price, that of systematically excluding the great variation among the aged from consideration? In particular, since it is well known that only a small proportion of the elderly have very high health-care costs and needs, why not focus our rationing efforts on them? By limiting life-extending care to everyone, would we not indiscriminately sweep up many in otherwise fine shape who, with one or two timely medical interventions, might have remaining a number of years of good life? The answer is that we would indeed, in a sense, penalize the latter group; or more precisely, we would not benefit them, despite the fact that they would gain much more from life-extending treatment than those in poor condition. But I see no way to avoid, at some point, a choice that will cause anguish, shorten some lives, and possibly appear unjust.[3]

Callahan is not interested only in financial issues, for he claims that this rationing system comports with a proper understanding of the nature of the good life. Mandatory, universal, age-based rationing of scarce medical resources is an ethically upright proposal because after one reaches the end of one's natural lifespan, attaining the good life becomes increasingly difficult. The ill health, pain, loneliness, impoverishment, and growing debilitation of the elderly make the good life more difficult to attain, though not impossible for the elderly.

Callahan is not claiming that the lives of the elderly are without value, but only that the good life is more difficult to attain, which makes efforts to promote and preserve it futile: "Only later was I to visit a nursing home and to learn even more, about old age as a time of crushing physical and emotional burdens for some time, and life as a trouble to be endured until the release of death." Life in itself is not an independent good, for it must be accompanied by other values to be worth sustaining: "good health and long life are still not quite enough. What good are they if old age cannot be a time of satisfaction, continued personal fulfillment, and social respect." Aging "has forever been one of those problems acceptable for some, but fearsome for most."[4]

Because of the diminished abilities of the elderly to live the good life, Callahan states that the goal of medicine is to "help the aged maintain a physical and psychological life sufficient to enhance the realization of those aspirations; that is, not more life as such, but a life free of whatever pain and suffering might impede these ends."[5] The lives of the elderly have value, but it becomes difficult to justify the burdens of supporting such lives because of the diminished prospects for living the good life:

> the difficulties of caring for the elderly display three unique features. The first is the increasingly endemic nature of their illnesses, which are less curable than they are controllable. The price of an extended life span for the elderly is an increase in chronic illness. The second feature follows from the first: the sheer number and proportion of the elderly as a pool of ill or impaired people. The third is the growing necessity to make painful moral choices in the care of the elderly dying as a class, particularly among those who end their days incompetent and grossly incapacitated, more dead than alive.[6]

Callahan asserts that for some of the elderly, there can be a "tolerable death": "death at the end of a long and full life is not an evil, that indeed there is something fitting and orderly about it." A tolerable death is one where:

a)   one's life possibilities have on the whole been accomplished;

b)   one's moral obligations to those for whom one has had responsibility have been discharged; and,

c)   one's death will not seem to others an offense to sense or sensibility or tempt others to despair and rage about the finitude of human existence.[7]

When these conditions are met, life ceases to be good, and, relative to death, it becomes an evil. For Callahan, the value and good of life become situationally dependent, and he does not regard human life as always being a good for the person, for it can be a burden in some situations, and, when so, no harm is done to the person when that life is destroyed. To destroy a life that is not a benefit to a person is not to do a harm, but rather is to do a good to the person. He regards death rather benignly, stating that in old age it becomes one's friend, and for the old and very old, death is not the ultimate enemy, but a friend.

Callahan takes a radical view not only of aging, life, and death, but also of intergenerational obligations, the role of the state, and of the rights of individuals.

Toward "Medical Totalitarianism"

Callahan's proposal addresses the intersection of life and death, law, individual rights, and economic and financing issues. He recognizes that rationing health care resources is a dirty and unpleasant business, only made tolerable if all are required to take equal risks. He resolves these conflicts by preventing a certain class from receiving any financial support or health care whatsoever. But his resolution is obviously not voluntary, liberal, or democratic. Indeed, he denies individual freedom or personal right to exempt one's self from the program. Such a rationing system would be elective only in the sense that an electorate could vote it into existence, but with the elderly in a minority, mandatory, age-based rationing could easily degenerate into a tyranny of the younger generations against the elderly. It is a system that could be rather easily imposed by the young on the elderly against their will, and for the elderly, age-based rationing would be a highly coercive system.

For Callahan, allowing exceptions to medical resource rationing would be intolerable because that would impose greater burdens on some classes than on others and would be analogous to permitting exemptions from military conscription. Callahan does not mention that the mandatory and universal character of his program violates the personal rights and consciences of many individuals, and he considers its universal and mandatory character a virtue because it supposedly does not unduly burden anyone.

Even if individuals claim a moral right in conscience to receive inexpensive, effective, and nonpainful medical care, he would not allow this to happen to prevent others from being unduly burdened. His absolute refusal to give anything except analgesia to the elderly is more all-encompassing than was American military conscription in this century, for even in that system conscientious objectors were traditionally not required to participate in armed service. Rather than being a rationing system based on liberal and democratic principles, it is a totalitarian and coercive system of health care resource allocation.

His "medical totalitarianism" is even broader. Not only are those who have outlived their natural lifespan prohibited from seeking any care except analgesia, but Callahan would not permit health care providers to give them care from motives of conscience in any circumstance. Enacting this sort of prohibition would be most extraordinary, for virtually every serious medical resource rationing scheme allows for some exemptions for reasons of conscience. But he would not allow a physician or health care facility to treat, with or without compensation, those living beyond their natural lifespan, as this would create exceptions and make others bear undue burdens.

He denies that he is in favor of euthanasia, but in practice his program would promote widespread, involuntary elimination of the sick elderly by omission:

> So many, indeed, are the attractions of euthanasia and assisted suicide that it might seem obvious for me to commend them as part of a policy of limiting life extension for the elderly.
>
> My conclusion is exactly the opposite: a sanctioning of mercy killing and assisted suicide for the elderly would offer them little practical help and would serve as a threatening symbol of devaluation of old age. I want to be clear about my argument here. I will not develop a full account of the problem of euthanasia and assisted suicide; that is beyond the scope of this book (though I will say that I oppose it).[8]

These denials do not speak loudly, however, for he admits there would be circumstances in which the wishes of patients would have to be overridden. The urgent necessity to limit spending and eliminate those whose lives have made expenditure of medical resources less valuable makes this imperative. And rather than morally defending involuntary withdrawal of inexpensive medical care from the elderly, he proclaims that the old "would have to understand that the intent behind a policy of limiting care would be the welfare of the elderly and of younger generations, and that it was affirmative toward old age and not simply mean-spirited. The young would have to understand that while their own eventual old age would be marked by limits of a kind not earlier experienced by the elderly, they would on balance have a better old age than was earlier the case."[9]

If the principles underlying this proposal were applied to pregnant teenagers addicted to crack cocaine, they would yield exceedingly disturbing results. With these cases where life and death, law, individual liberties, and financing health care converge, they would require unmarried, crack-addicted mothers to abort and no individual would be permitted to abstain from having the required abortion. Many of these unmarried teenage cocaine users would want to abort their babies, but others would not, and they would be forced to do so under medical totalitarianism. At the present time, there are nearly 10,000 crack babies in our country costing millions of dollars and their prospects for a full and rich life are not good.[10] The high cost of supporting these children, the urgent need to curb unwanted teenage pregnancies, and the diminished possibilities available to such children to live the good life all make this policy necessary.

Morally, there are no relevant differences between these two cases, and the application of Callahan's principles would require involuntary abortion of crack babies. Both the elderly and pregnant crack women are full citizens possessing specific constitutional rights. In Callahan's view, neither the elderly nor pregnant teenage crack addicts have much potential to make major contributions to society, and both present significant burdens to their families. Strict application of Callahan's principles would mandate health care providers to perform or cooperate with the abortions on all crack babies, regardless of a specific mother's wishes.

This application of Callahan's principles makes it rather clear that age-based rationing is neither liberal nor tolerant, but is medical totalitarianism. This quality is seen even more clearly in his most recent book, *What Kind of Life,* in which he declares that the state must use its power to enforce both his age-based rationing proposal and his theory of the good life.[11] The use of state power is necessary because not all citizens in our republic are accustomed to such blunt use of force and because such a scheme would require massive reeducation of the public in the nature of the good life, at least as Callahan defines it. Individuals would have to be persuaded that the elderly have little possibility of attaining the good life and that they have "positive" obligations not to consume medical resources "reserved" for the young.

Callahan considers his system to be egalitarian and democratic because all would bear the burdens equally and because initiation of such a system would be the result of a free, popular vote. But this allocation system is antidemocratic because it unduly burdens politically outnumbered and weaker citizens (the elderly) to benefit more numerous and more powerful younger citizens. This program is contrary to the ideals of a liberal democracy that seeks to distribute burdens equally and to protect the politically weak and outnumbered from bearing undue burdens imposed for the benefit of the majority.

Age-Based Rationing and Value Inversion

In a most ingenious manner, Callahan's system inverts a number of critical moral values and makes what were previously vices and evils into values and virtues. For him, old age is a time when the good life becomes more difficult. Age-based rationing is beneficial to the elderly because it frees them from unrealistic expectations about living and it prohibits the elderly from imposing unacceptable burdens on younger generations. It emancipates the elderly from the illusion that old age is a time of uninterrupted rest, peace, and enjoyment without suffering, anxiety, or loneliness and reveals their responsibilities to the young. And this reformed vision of old age at a time of uncertainty and doubt compels Callahan to invert all of the values associated with old age.

In the preinverted morality the young had duties to the elderly because the elderly gave them life, supported, and protected them. But in Callahan's value-inverted moral universe, the elderly have an obligation to the young not to consume the medical resources the young need. There is little mention in his value inversion of the obligation of the young to compensate the elderly for their years of service, but only of the obligation of the elderly not to consume goods supposedly reserved for the young.

Callahan's view of society is one that is less tolerant of the diverse views of consciences and less willing to accept moral heterogeneity than is contemporary society. His scheme can tolerate no deviations from or exceptions to his system, and the ideals of tolerance and pluralism are inverted in the name of equal sharing of burdens that transforms radical intolerance into a virtue. Callahan subordinates all moral and professional codes to age-based rationing, does not permit any other value to compromise the comprehensive and mandatory nature of his scheme, and precludes all other approaches to the problem. His system overturns traditional respect for the autonomy and independence of informed, morally responsible medical judgment, and he makes it the servant of economic emergency and the new perspective on the nature of old age.

Callahan's system abandons the traditional confidence in educated and free moral agents to manage a community without coercion. In his moral universe individuals are unable to respond adequately to this financial crisis, and the state must employ coercion to save us from disaster. He has abandoned the view that individuals in a democratic society can freely achieve a consensus to curb costs without the coercive intervention of the state. And the classical view that the individual agent should be responsible for preserving and promoting his or her health is overturned: in his system it is the state that assumes this responsibility.

Callahan's system also inverts traditional views of equality. Equality had implied a balance, giving for what one had received or providing in order to have something given in return.[12] But Callahan's equality excludes these considerations. For him, equality means that the elderly forego all care and life-sustaining treatment, not because they have overused the health care system and owe these resources to others, but because their rightful use might deprive the young of these resources. In spite of what Callahan claims, the elderly have a title to inexpensive, minimal, beneficial, and nonpainful health care, but only because they have the responsibility to take reasonable measures to promote their health and well-being.

But Callahan imposes on the elderly a duty to abstain from promoting their own health and well-being so that they can foster the health and well-being of others. The elderly receive no benefits for the burdens they incur by foregoing all care and treatment, while the younger receive access to greater medical resources and incur no obligations to the elderly by reason of their increased consumption of those resources. Relative to the benefits won by the younger, the elderly are uncompensated for their losses, presumably suffered against their will in many instances.

In Callahan's views of equality, the debt traditionally owed by the young to the elderly is transformed into a claim against them. More conventional morality believed that the elderly had a claim to some of the resources of the young because they had sheltered and cared for them, but Callahan's inversion gives the young a claim against the elderly because their use of medical resources burdens the young. Most of the elderly have suffered significant losses of freedom to support, care for, protect, and educate the young, but under Callahan's proposal, the young would not be required to accept similar losses of freedom or financial resources to provide similar care, shelter, and protection for the elderly. Callahan claims his scheme protects equality, but his system actually perpetuates and protects gross inequities and injustices. The elderly are required to support the young and are then compelled to step aside when no longer needed because the young consider their support insufficiently beneficial in relation to the costs of the care.

Callahan claims that his proposal imposes equal burdens on all, but, in fact, the burdens and benefits are not equally distributed even among the elderly. If such a system were to be fully responsive to the demands of equality, it would have to compensate some of the elderly more fully than others because the moderately ill elderly who would die from denial of minimal care would suffer a greater loss than would those dying from the withdrawal of more costly and burdensome care. Classical notions of equality would demand that these less seriously ill elders be given greater compensation for their deaths, but this is not allowed in Callahan's system. These elderly who are less ill would require little care or treatment to continue living, but being denied that minimal benefit, they would suffer a greater loss than would others. If one is going to base age-based rationing on considerations of equality, it would be imperative that the elderly be given greater compensation because they suffer greater losses than others.

Age-Based Rationing: An Unworkable Proposal

Totalitarian, age-based rationing would be unworkable and impossible to administer. Many elders would not accept such a coercive, discriminatory program that so disregarded the rights of conscience. They would obtain medical care by deception. Many elders would flock to those health care facilities that refused to participate in the system or offered care because of reasons of conscience, and those health care systems willing to offer care could profit from these patients, while those who did not would lose these profits.

Most physicians would not tolerate a system that denied care on purely economic and nonmedical grounds. Many would object to another intrusion of the state into medical practice. Physicians who regard patient well-being as their primary concern would argue that denying effective and available care to balance ledgers and promote cost-effectiveness would impair their reputations and practice. Health care providers could rightly claim that they would be unduly inhibited in their medical practice because they would not be allowed to treat the elderly according to their conscientious judgments. They would object that such a program would force them to practice personally repugnant forms of medicine, for they would be compelled in the name of equality to deny care and treatment to those who had a rightful claim to it.

We already know that most abortionists are ostracized by medical professionals,[13] and those physicians who refused to treat readily correctable conditions simply because the patient is old might well be similarly shunned. Under such a medical regime, physicians would be reluctant to specialize in gerontology if they would be forced to terminate care whenever their patients reach the end of their so-called natural lifespan.

Coercive, universal, age-based rationing would signal the end of aggressive gerontological research, for there would be little incentive to develop new therapeutic protocols for the old and very old. In many health care institutions, life-saving resources might be available but could not be used simply because the patients needing them would be too old. And many health care professionals might find it impossible to stand aside while seniors died and medicines and other life-saving means were unused.

Such a rationing scheme does not confront the difficulties involved in its administration. Wealthy physicians who would favor treating the elderly would not tolerate being forced to tell them that they could not be treated because they have been arbitrarily determined to be too old or because there is too little money. Envision a scenario similar to the following:

> *Dr. Bob:* I am sorry, Mrs. Smith, but we cannot insert a gastrostomy tube to feed you because you are seventy-nine years old and you do not qualify for this sort of care. We will give you pain killers and ice chips to keep you comfortable as you starve and dehydrate to death.
>
> *Mrs. Smith:* But, Doctor, I can pay for this. You have the devices, the surgical suites, and the staff available to do this. I will die if you do not perform this simple procedure.
>
> *Dr. Bob:* I realize that, Mrs. Smith, but this is now national medical policy. I can't discuss it now. I have to leave for lunch at the country club.

Callahan gives little thought to who would inform elderly patients that they could not receive any more medical care. If physicians were not given this task, who would do it? Would nurses or hospital staff? Would it be passed to government bureaucrats? And if members of any of these groups would have to be the harbingers of death, how would people be recruited for such tasks?

On the surface, Callahan's system has the advantage of simplicity, for it would be automatically activated when an individual reached an arbitrarily determined age. However, mandatory, universal, age-based rationing would prove practically unworkable because it would create a two-tiered system permitting the wealthy to receive medical treatment through an underground health care network while denying it to the poor. For it is inconceivable that courts would convict elders or health care providers for seeking or providing minimal care.

A compulsory, universal, age-based rationing system would encourage corruption, bribery, and black market medicine, and such a system would be dangerous to the elderly who would probably travel far and wide in search of health care. Many elders would feel morally compelled to lie about their age or bribe hospitals and physicians to treat them. Many health care providers would be unwilling to enforce its requirements strictly, and physicians would often accept paying elderly patients who needed minimal care and who would die without it. Callahan's universal, compulsory, age-based rationing system would deny care to those who could benefit from it and who would not be a financial burden to the system because they could pay for their care. And such an age-based system would do nothing to curb immoderate use of the health care system by those who have not lived past their natural lifespan.

It is quite possible that a mandatory and universal age-based system for the elderly would have no significant influence on medical expenditures because nothing in this allocation system would curb excessive use of health care resources by the younger members of society. For younger citizens could spend lavishly on health care during their natural lifespan, and these excessive expenditures might not be compensated for by the economizing of the elderly. In the end, Callahan's system might only succeed in killing off a large number of elders who could have lived with minimal care or treatment and not affect any significant reduction of expenditures because the younger would not be inhibited at all in their health care spending.

Conclusion

Callahan selects age as the basis for rationing medical treatments and care, even though many elderly persons can live for years if given minimal care and medical treatment. The medical efficacy of care and treatment is not as important as is the age of the person receiving the care or treatment. This is discriminatory because it invokes conditions over which the elderly have no control (their age) to deny them services from which they can derive as much benefit as others. It is as discriminatory as would be a rationing system that denied medical care to persons because of their race or nationality.

It has long been recognized that there are many legitimate criteria for allocating medical resources, and Callahan does not explain why age should be the critical factor in constituting a valid title to health care benefits other than that he sees his scheme as more fair than others. Other systems use other criteria: first-come, first-served; need; ability to pay; social utility; the length and quality of one's service to society; plight of those dependent on the recipient.[14] Recognizing these and other alternatives is important because a mandatory, comprehensive, age-based rationing system does not manifest significantly greater justice, fairness, or utility than do these other options. Callahan's proposal would overturn the classical standards for providing care and medical treatment and deny elderly patients effective, inexpensive, and relatively painless care.[15]

His ostensible justification for the coercive and universally binding character of this program is not the greater futility of providing care for those who have less opportunity to live the good life, but appears to be the impending financial collapse of our health care system. If Callahan were only concerned with the diminished ability of the elderly to live the good life, there would not be the urgency to withhold care from them. The suspension of rights of conscience and the mandatory, universal character of the program are mandated solely because he sees the present situation has reached a crisis stage. But if this so-called emergency justifies suspension of individual rights, what other rights can be suspended in the face of other more pressing emergencies?

Despite Callahan's claims, all persons are responsible for taking reasonable care of their health and life, regardless of their age, and they must be allowed use of whatever inexpensive, nonpainful, and effective life-sustaining measures are available to fulfill that responsibility.[16] This is not to say that everyone is to have access to expensive or potentially futile treatment to sustain their lives, but that everyone must use what is clinically effective and readily available to sustain their lives, irrespective of the age. This would ordinarily mean that one would have to have adequate sleep, nutrition, exercise, shelter, clothing, and minimal medical care. Callahan's proposal is morally objectionable because it denies the elderly the means to act responsibly toward the good of their health and life. The duty to take care remains binding on the elderly, but Callahan's system would deny them the means to fulfill this duty.

NOTES

1. Daniel Callahan, *Setting Limits: Medical Goals in an Aging Society* (New York: Simon and Schuster, 1987).

2. Ibid., 171, 137–38. Callahan does not state explicitly that he prohibits exceptions, but he admits that coercing the elderly could have negative connotations. However, he is willing to accept that as an evil more tolerable than other evils, and he does not shy away from the use of coercion because he sees no other superior alternative (197–99).

3. Ibid., 155.

4. Ibid., 14, 19.

5. Ibid., 53. The implication clearly is that a life lacking these capabilities does not deserve even minimal support.

6. Ibid., 117–18.

7. Ibid., 65, 66.

8. Ibid., 194.

9. Ibid., 199–200.

10. ABC News, Mar. 7, 1990.

11. Daniel Callahan, *What Kind of Life: The Limits of Medical Progress* (New York: Simon and Schuster, 1990).

12. Thomas Aquinas, *Summa Theologica*, II–II, Q. 58, 10, Resp.

13. "Under Pressure and Stigma, More Doctors Shun Abortion," *New York Times*, Jan. 8, 1990, A1.

14. Gene Outka, "Social Justice and Equal Access to Health Care," *Journal of Religious Ethics* 2, no. 1 (Spring 1974): 11–32.

15. Callahan rejects the medical need standard that allocates health care, believing that need is "too elastic a concept." See Callahan, *Setting Limits,* 138. He also believes that "no technology should be developed or applied to the elderly that does not promise *great* [italics mine] and inexpensive improvement in the quality of their lives, no matter how promising for life extension. Incremental gains, achieved at high cost, should be considered unacceptable" (143).

16. See Thomas O'Donnell, *Medicine and Christian Morality* (New York: Alba House, 1971), 54–55.

2

Life as an Evil; Death as a Good: Dualism and Callahan's Inversion

ROBERT P. GEORGE

Daniel Callahan, director and cofounder of the Hastings Center and one of America's leading medical ethicists, has proposed that as a matter of public policy we should settle on a "natural" lifespan after which medical care should no longer be used to extend the lives of elderly people, but only to relieve their suffering. Callahan's proposal has provoked legal and medical scholars, philosophers, policy analysts, and specialists in other academic and professional disciplines to think seriously about the problem of allocating scarce medical resources in a society whose proportion of older to younger citizens is growing. Callahan does not, however, wish to rest his case for an age-based standard for terminating life-extending health care exclusively on the claim that intergenerational fairness and/or prudence requires that we allocate scarce resources that could be used for life-extending care for the elderly to meet the medical and other needs of younger people. His claim is, as he puts it, "more austere": the extension of life beyond a certain age "is neither a wise social goal nor one that the aged themselves should want, however compellingly it will attract them."[1]

I focus on this thesis in criticizing Callahan's proposal, and I begin by explaining the traditional understanding of the morality of relieving suffering by means that hasten death. I intend to show that Callahan inverts traditional casuistry and that implicit in this inversion is a rejection of the traditional understanding of life as an intrinsic good and death as always in itself an evil. Finally, I argue that the dualistic premises of Callahan's rejection of the traditional understanding are untenable.

According to traditional casuistry, one may, for the sake of relieving the suffering of a dying patient, licitly administer a palliative whose unintended but foreseeable side effect is the shortening of life. However, one may not intend death, even as a means of relieving suffering. Traditional casuistry presupposes an idea that certain critics of traditional morality deny, namely, that one need not intend (in the morally relevant sense of intend) all the foreseeable consequences of one's choices.

Common sense, however, vindicates this presupposition and confounds its critics: one simply does not intend that curtains will fade when one knowingly hangs them in the sunlight, for example, or that running shoes will wear out when one knowingly uses them. One accepts the fading or wearing out as a side effect of one's choice to hang the curtains or wear the shoes. One can, to be sure, be morally responsible for the side effects one accepts or refuses to accept, but one will be morally responsible in a different way from that in which one is morally responsible for consequences one intends.

It is important to notice that the distinction between "intending" and "accepting side effects" does not track the distinction between acts and omissions (though the latter distinction can, in some circumstances, be relevant to moral reasoning). One may intend death, for example, by acting or, in certain circumstances, by declining to act. One's intention is defined by what one chooses; and to choose is, essentially, to adopt a proposal that one has put to oneself in one's practical deliberation. What one intends, then, is whatever is included in the proposal one adopts; and something can be included in one's proposal either as an end in itself or as a means to an end.

Of course, one may or may not *desire* what one intends, especially what one intends as a means. It is simply a mistake, albeit a common one, to suppose that human choices and actions necessarily manifest the dominant desires of human agents. This mistaken position, the source of familiar forms of reductionism in the social and behavioral sciences, manifests a denial of the reality of free choice; for choice can be free, in a morally meaningful sense, when it is between rationally appealing, incompatible practical proposals when no factor but the choosing itself settles which alternative is chosen.[2]

One chooses freely, in the morally relevant sense, only when one has ultimate (or basic) reasons for action. The possibility of free choice thus presupposes the possibility of rationally motivated action. One acts on a rational motive where one chooses for the sake of a reason whose intelligibility does not depend on the intelligibility of still deeper reasons or on subrational factors (such as emotional motives). Only something understood to be an end in itself is capable of providing an ultimate reason for action.

The intelligibility of ultimate reasons for action, qua ultimate, cannot be deduced, inferred, or, in any strict sense, derived from anything else. One grasps the intelligibility of ultimate reasons, if at all, without the benefit of deductions, inferences, or derivations. Thomas Aquinas concluded, therefore, that such reasons, which provide the first principles of practical thinking and action, are per se nota (self-evident) and indemonstrabilia. But here Aquinas is easily misunderstood: he did not suppose, and we should not imagine, that it is impossible to be mistaken about self-evident practical principles. An act of understanding—an insight—is required to grasp any intelligibility, whether the intelligibility of a self-evident reason for action or anything else. Many of the factors that may impede or deflect understanding with respect to derived propositions may also impede or deflect the insights required for the rational affirmation of self-evident truths. Anyone can fail to grasp a self-evident proposition, just as anyone can fail to understand a valid deduction. By the same token, a self-evident proposition remains true (and self-evident) even if someone (or, indeed, everyone) fails to grasp it. And it goes without saying that sometimes propositions that people claim to be self-evident turn out to state-derived (and therefore not self-evident) truths or even to be false.

There are many ultimate reasons for action. Many human ends or purposes, including friendships, knowledge, recreation, artistic performances and their critical appreciation, authenticity, and integrity are capable of motivating action and providing a nonbaffling answer to the question "Why would anybody do that?" These human ends or purposes are not merely instrumentally valuable; they are intelligibly worth achieving, or realizing, or participating in just for their own sakes. Unlike, say, money, to take the standard example of a purely instrumental good, one can intelligibly pursue friendship, knowledge, beauty, and the like not merely for their extrinsic benefits but also for their intrinsic worth. As intrinsic goods, they are constitutive aspects of the persons in whom they are instantiated.

Traditional morality holds that among the intrinsic human goods are the goods of life and health. Like other intrinsic goods, these goods provide certain instrumental benefits. Bodily life is a condition for the realization of any other human good; and health is a condition for the full enjoyment of other goods. According to the tradition, however, life and health are not *merely* instrumental because they are not extrinsic to the persons in whom they are instantiated. Rather, they are intrinsic and, therefore, partially constitutive aspects of persons.

The status of life and health as intrinsic goods grounds the traditional casuists' principle that one may never licitly intend death, whether as end or means. The point goes to the foundation of moral reasoning. Morality, according to the tradition, is about rectitude in willing. In choosing—that is, in adopting a proposal—one's will is, in a sense, synthesized with the proposal one adopts. Thus, one establishes one's own character—one constitutes one's moral self—in one's free choices. One becomes, in a sense, what one has set one's will (i.e., intended) to do.

In its self-constituting aspect, the voluntariness of intention is radically unlike every other form of voluntariness, including, notably, that form of voluntariness involved in knowingly causing side effects. No other form of voluntariness can accomplish the self-constitution that cannot be avoided in the forming of an intention.

Now, if ultimate reasons for action were commensurable—that is, if they could be weighed against each other according to a common standard—it might be possible to conclude that intending death, whether by act or omission, is sometimes morally justified. As I have observed, there are many ultimate reasons for action, many basic human goods; and no one doubts that sometimes it is possible to advance one basic good by intending, as a means, the destruction of another. Thus, some contemporary consequentialist moral thinkers claim that many actions condemned in principle by traditional morality, including certain actions involving an intention to kill, are sometimes morally permissible precisely because the values served by such action outweigh the values damaged.

The difficulty with all forms of consequentialism is that ultimate reasons for action are, in reality, *in*commensurable. Contemporary critics of consequentialism have shown that no objective standard exists for comparing the intrinsic value of knowledge with friendship, beauty with recreation, or one life with another or even ten or a hundred or a thousand others.[3] "Good" is predicated of ultimate reasons for action not univocally, i.e., in the same sense, but analogically; what basic goods have in common is precisely—and only—their status as ultimate reasons for action (reasons that are reducible neither to each other nor to some common underlying reality—e.g., some nonnatural quality called "goodness"). The apparent commensurability of values is therefore an illusion. The incommensurability of values is a fatal fact for situational ethics, and, indeed, for all theories that would make moral decisions depend on a comparison of (premoral) values. Choice and action in respect of the range of basic human goods must be guided, therefore, by nonconsequentialist norms of morality.

Traditional moralists hold that one of these norms excludes as practically unreasonable (i.e., immoral) any proposal to destroy, damage, or impede an intrinsic human good. This norm forbids us from intending death, whether as an end (e.g., out of hatred for the person whose life it is) or as a means (e.g., as a method of relieving suffering). Acting on a proposal to relieve suffering, however, by means that have the shortening of life among their consequences is not forbidden by this norm when death lies outside the scope of one's intention. So long as one does not *intend* death, and violates no norm applicable to the accepting of side effects (for example, a norm requiring one to act fairly and with a due regard for the welfare of others), one may administer a life-shortening palliative to a dying patient without immorality.

So far, I have been outlining the traditional casuistry controlling crucial decisions about deathbed care. I now wish to turn to Callahan's proposed age-based criterion for terminating medical care. I shall try to show that Callahan's position deviates from traditional morality far more radically than Callahan himself seems to suppose; and I shall argue that traditional morality is rationally superior to the new morality embodied in Callahan's proposal.

To begin with, Callahan confuses the distinction between intending death and accepting death as a side effect, on the one hand, with the distinction between inducing death and withholding care that could prevent death, on the other. The morally relevant distinction in the cases Callahan is interested in is the former and the withholding of care he proposes amounts in most cases to intending death.

More egregiously, Callahan inverts the traditional casuistry in arguing that after a certain age, continued life, rather than death, is the evil that one may accept as a foreseen but unintended side effect of a choice to relieve suffering (by means of unavoidably life-extending palliatives). This inversion is, moreover, no stray bullet, but is precisely determined by the trajectory set by Callahan's submerged but central premise: the proposition that persons are not their bodies but merely inhabit them. He does not defend this dualistic conception of the human person, but rather assumes it. To be sure, he holds well back from taking dualism to what many believe to be its ultimate conclusion, namely, that active, voluntary (and, even nonvoluntary) euthanasia is morally justifiable and ought to be legally permitted. But he is left with merely pragmatic arguments against such euthanasia.

Traditional morality, by contrast, rejects dualism for what I shall argue are compelling reasons. The nondualistic premises of traditional moral theory allow for principled arguments against euthanasia, and other forms of direct killing, on the ground that it is intrinsically wrong to intend death either as an end in itself or as a means to an end. If dualism is false, these arguments tell not only against forms of killing that Callahan opposes, but also against the withholding of care he proposes.

Callahan contends that his proposal to terminate medical care for those who live beyond the span of years settled upon as the "natural" lifespan is not discriminatory or "ageist." He invites us to imagine a society that understands the true goals of medicine and the true meaning of aging, a society with a renewed understanding of the life cycle, a society in which the elderly are respected for their wisdom and acknowledged to have a distinctive and important social role. In such a society, he avers, there would be nothing unfair to the elderly in his age-based proposal for withholding life-extending medical care.[4] True, in such a society persons who had lived out their allotted span of life might nevertheless *want* to go on living, but they would have *no right* to the medical resources necessary for them to ward off death. In such a society only persons who had not yet reached the legal age limit could claim those resources for the purpose of life extension.

Why is it that withholding the resources necessary to extend life from older members of the community does not represent an unfair disfavoring of their interests compared to the interests of younger members? Callahan's answer is murky. Perhaps it has something to do with the fact that everyone who is old was once young and therefore enjoyed the benefits of his scheme of allocation before being required to bear its burdens. I would suggest, however, that what is really doing the work here is Callahan's not-quite-explicit claim that, beyond a certain number of years (and individuals' desires to go on living notwithstanding), people just do not have a legitimate or rational interest in being (or staying) alive. Death, not life, serves the true interests of the oldest of the old. So, in refusing to permit them to draw on medical resources to extend their lives, we are not disfavoring their interests; to the contrary, we are favoring them. Reasoning along these line seems to lie behind Callahan's statement that "there is an important difference between taking age into account in order to provide the most appropriate treatment and the use of age as a standard for the discriminatory denial or modification of treatment."[5]

If, however, people beyond a certain age have an interest in death and not life, why not serve that interest fully and expeditiously by killing them? Advocates of active euthanasia and assisted suicide will surely press this question. On these issues Callahan's position closely resembles traditional morality. He opposes active euthanasia and would authorize the cessation of nutrition and hydration in few cases other than those exceptionally rare ones in which cessation might also be authorized by traditional casuists, namely, in cases in which the means of administering food and water are themselves profoundly and painfully burdensome. In the course of his discussion of nutrition and hydration, Callahan implies that his own under-standing of the morality of terminating care is not far from that of tradi-tional moralists. In generally opposing the withholding of nutrition and hydration, he says that "because it will be the specific cause of death . . . [the withholding of food and water] will have the appearance of direct killing rather than merely allowing to die."[6]

The notion of "direct" killing (as opposed to indirectly causing death) is drawn straight from traditional moral philosophy. According to the tradition, direct killing of the innocent is always wrong, but indirectly causing death may be morally legitimate. The tradition, however, manifestly does not distinguish direct from indirect by reference to the distinction between acts and omissions. The relevant distinction is, rather, between modes of voluntariness: one violates the moral norm against direct killing when one *intends* death, whether as end or means and whether by act or omission; one does not violate this norm (though one may violate other norms) when one accepts death as a *side effect.* "Allowing to die" may be morally permissible where the shortening of life, though foreseeable, lies outside the scope of one's intention. However, a choice to withhold life-saving treatment *precisely for the sake of hastening death* (even where death is sought, not as an end in itself, but as a means to the relief of suffering), despite being an omission (in common parlance "allowing to die"), violates the norm against intending death. In short, "allowing to die" may be a form of direct killing.

In proposing to withhold life-extending care from the eldest of the elderly, Callahan supposes that he is not proposing killing them but merely "allowing them to die." Most telling in this regard is his willingness to withhold even antibiotics from the aged. He says that "pneumonia should be allowed to become, once again, 'the old man's friend.' "[7] If he understands "allowing to die" in this sense to be consistent with the traditional norm against direct killing, he is gravely mistaken. The withholding of nonburdensome medications precisely for the sake of hastening death *is* direct killing. It is *intending* death, albeit as a means and by omission. It is anything but accepting death as a side effect. Death is the very point of the choice, the "good" that is intended by someone deciding to withhold medication; death is not treated as an evil that must be accepted as a foreseen but unintended consequence of action whose point is to achieve some other good (e.g., the relief of suffering).

Callahan could have defended his age-based proposal for allocating health care purely by appealing to intergenerational fairness. He might then have argued that in withholding scarce medical resources from those least likely to benefit from them and most likely to have gotten a fair shot at life's opportunities already, we are not intending the foreseeable deaths of those from whom resources would be withheld, but merely (and without injustice) accepting their deaths as unintended side effects. Such an argument might or might not have been persuasive. The proposed allocation principle might or might not be distributively fair. (As I have already implied, I doubt that it would be.) Callahan, however, explicitly and forcefully declines to defend his proposal by appealing to intergenerational fairness or even to economic prudence; he is committed to the "more austere" thesis.

Nowhere is the austerity of this thesis more striking than in Callahan's inversion of the traditional casuistry of deathbed treatment decisions. Noting that "medical efforts to relieve suffering will frequently have the unintended but foreseeable consequence of extending life expectancy," he declares that it is nonetheless permissible, even required, to relieve suffering and accept the extension of life as a side effect. "Under no circumstances would it be acceptable to fail to relieve suffering because of the possibility of life extension."[8]

For the traditional casuist, life is an intrinsic good, death an evil. Suffering (also an evil) may be alleviated by means that do not implicate a choice to set one's will against the good of life. Where death is outside the scope of one's intention, however, it may be accepted as a foreseen but unintended side effect of the effort to alleviate suffering. Where no unfairness or other species of immorality attends the acceptance of death, one is not morally responsible for bringing about death, even if death was among the probable or even certain consequences of one's choice to administer the palliative.

In Callahan's inversion of the traditional casuistry, suffering is still an evil. But for someone who has lived a natural lifespan, life is no longer a good, so death can no longer be an evil. It is rather the reverse. Death may remain emotionally "an occasion for sadness" (as he sometimes says), but life is no longer a reason for action. Death, rather, is a reason for inaction (or omission). To be sure, Callahan remains opposed to active euthanasia, and even to a certain type of killing by omission, namely, that involving the withholding of nutrition and hydration. Nothing morally relevant, however, turns on the distinction between acts and omissions here: what one intends in withholding medical care is death—the avoidance of death, i.e., the extension of life, is acceptable only as a side effect; it may not be licitly intended as if it were a reason for action, a good.

Consistent with his inversion of the traditional understanding of the value of life and the evil of death in certain circumstances, Callahan's arguments against euthanasia and assisted suicide are pragmatic. He does not argue that directly killing (even by *his* definition of "directly") those whom he would "allow to die" is wrong in principle. Rather, he maintains that "mercy killing and assisted suicide for the elderly would offer them little help and would serve as a threatening symbol of devaluation of old age."[9] Now I do not mean to suggest that this argument is without merit; but one should not expect the leadership of the Hemlock Society to lose any sleep over it. If fear of the symbolism or message of euthanasia were the only or most powerful argument against it, one could imagine effective schemes for socializing people from their earliest years to appreciate the profound blessing of a conveniently timed and painlessly executed death. Indeed, advocates of euthanasia might borrow Callahan's own strategy and argue that their program would be appropriate only in a morally transformed society in which the elderly were properly esteemed. In such a society, the elderly would feel secure in the knowledge that their true interests were foremost in the minds of those who would end their lives.

I have claimed that Callahan's inversion of traditional casuistry reflects an inversion of the traditional understanding of the value of life and the evil of death. He certainly treats the extension of life, beyond a certain number of years, as an undesirable side effect that may be accepted in cases where suffering can only be relieved by drugs that, unavoidably, lengthen life. Presumably, were equally effective alternatives available, ones that did not extend life, he would consider these palliatives rationally preferable. I should pause here, however, to point out that Callahan's text is not without ambiguity. For example, near the beginning of a chapter entitled "Allocating Resources to the Elderly," he says: "My underlying intention is to affirm the inestimable value of individual human life, of the old as much as the young, and the value of old age as part of our individual and collective life. I must then meet a severe challenge: to propose a way of limiting resources to the elderly, and a spirit behind that way, which are compatible with that affirmation."[10]

Throughout *Setting Limits,* however, he castigates "the modernizers" for treating death as an enemy to be conquered. Moreover, in a chapter section entitled "Can There Be a Natural Life Span and a Tolerable Death?" he suggests that "death at the end of a long and full life is not an evil, that indeed there is something fitting and orderly about it."[11] To be sure, he subsequently disavows the belief that death in old age is an "unmitigated good," but he implies that what mitigates its value is an emotional factor: "it is a loss and the most ultimate kind of human loss." He asserts that "neither in the eyes of others nor in those of the elderly is death seen as an evil, even though it will be understood as a loss." And he allows that the "obvious premise behind [his] definition of a tolerable death and a natural life span is that such a death after such a life is not an evil, even though it may be an occasion for sadness."[12] Finally, he speaks freely of "the value of death," albeit only a paragraph before restating his belief that "life is precious."[13] He closes the section with a statement no one disputes but that contributes exactly nothing to his case—"one point should be evident: a longer and healthier old age will not provide the ultimate answer to death or remove its sting."[14] True. But the intelligible value of life in the elderly, no less than in the young, does not depend on its providing ultimate answers to death or removing its sting. If Callahan means to answer a counterargument about the value of life, he is beating a straw man.

If, as traditional morality holds, life is an intrinsic human good, Callahan's case for the age-based standard for terminating life-extending medical treatment collapses. But one cannot directly demonstrate that something is intrinsically valuable. As I have already observed, *ultimate* reasons for action, qua ultimate, cannot be deduced, inferred, or, in any strict sense, derived from deeper reasons. Such reasons are, in the technical sense I specified earlier, self-evident. So how are we to adjudicate the dispute between traditional morality and the new morality that Callahan, implicitly or explicitly, adopts? Do assertions of self-evidence terminate debate over primary practical principles? Must we conclude that either one immediately grasps the intrinsic value of life or one does not?

I think the debate can be adjudicated and that traditional morality prevails. While it is true that no direct argument can be given for the intrinsic value of life (or any other intrinsic value), indirect or dialectical arguments establish the falsity of the alternative proposition that life is only conditionally or instrumentally valuable. Dialectical arguments focus on the relationships between propositions (including putatively self-evident propositions) to be defended and other knowledge. Their point is to highlight the rationally unacceptable implications of denying the propositions to be defended, or the inappropriateness of relying on certain evidence (shown to be inapt or defective) to deny or cast doubt on these propositions. Retorsive arguments (arguments showing up the self-refuting quality of propositions such as "no sentence states a true proposition") are familiar forms of dialectical argumentation used to support self-evident propositions (such as the proposition that "knowledge is a good").

The proposition that bodily life is merely conditionally or instrumentally good implies that life is extrinsic to persons. Thus, this proposition implicates a particular position on what Callahan rightly calls "one of the oldest philosophical questions": the question of person/body dualism. Callahan usefully states the question as "whether we are our bodies or merely inhabit them."[15] Dualism claims that we merely inhabit them. Our bodies are not ourselves. They are instruments that we use. They serve our interests when they are functioning well, but become useless—or even worse—when they fall into permanent decay.

Medicine, on dualistic premises, should seek to preserve life and even to advance health only where these ends serve the higher, nonphysiological values of the true person, the person who merely inhabits a body. Joseph Fletcher, who self-consciously and unambiguously embraces dualism, argues for terminating medical treatment once a patient's cerebral function has ended on the ground that "nothing remains but biological phenomena at best. The patient is gone even if his body remains, and even if some of its vital functions continue."[16]

Nondualists are not necessarily materialists, though they may be. By the same token, dualists may be materialists, though they need not be. So the dispute between dualism and nondualism is not a version of the dispute about materialism. Nondualists may, as traditional morality does, affirm a range of irreducibly basic, incommensurable, intrinsic human values. Respect for persons understood in light of this axiology entails that one never intend to destroy any intrinsic human good instantiated in any human person. It does not always forbid acting for the sake of other goods in ways that, as side effects, damage the good of life. Were it otherwise, it would not only forbid the giving (or taking) of life-shortening palliatives, but it would also condemn every martyr as a suicide.

Callahan's argument presupposes dualism. But he nowhere formally endorses a dualistic position. In a number of places, however, he explicitly adopts a dualistic understanding of the person. He distinguishes sharply, and in a way meant to guide choice and action, between the needs of the patient as a person and the needs of "an assemblage of deficient organs."[17] He says that "the 'sanctity of life' has to be the sanctity of personhood, not merely the possession of a body." He distinguishes "biographical life" from "biological life" and holds that the former is of key moral concern. This distinction exactly parallels the dualistic distinction between the person and the body. He labels as "vitalism" "the view that life in itself, regardless of its condition, ought to be valued and preserved," and he endorses the contrary view that "the preservation of life should be determined by the condition of that life."[18] Finally, he holds that patients in a persistent vegetative state may be deprived even of nutrition and hydration, arguing that "they serve no purpose, and do no honor to the body or memory of the person who once inhabited that body." In these cases, he would provide nursing care only "out of the respect due human bodies prior to clinical death." In speaking of severely demented human beings, he again explicitly distinguishes persons from their bodies: "the death of the person, if not the body, is under way and need not be resisted" (though here he would continue to provide food and water).[19] Finally, he distinguishes a "mere," albeit living, body from "an embodied person."

Consistent with his dualistic position, Callahan treats the good of "health" as also a purely instrumental good (though, following Leon Kass, he says that it alone, and not life, is the true end of medicine). Callahan, in effect, denies that health is an *ultimate* intelligible reason for action. He says that "health itself, we sometimes need reminding, is a means and not an end. We can do nothing with good health itself; it makes other human goods possible."[20]

So Callahan embraces dualism more or less explicitly. What's wrong with that? Much.

First, if the human individual is a duality, how are the parts distinguishable? Where is the line between individual as end and as means? In fact, no line can be drawn, despite countless attempts by philosophers throughout history.

Second, life is not a process distinguishable from other processes like breathing, thinking, feeling pain, or making choices. Life is a pervasive reality. It is the living human being who breathes, converts nutrients into energy, thinks, feels pain, and makes choices.

If life is pervasive in these respects, however, then those activities that are unquestionably of intrinsic value for human beings, such as knowing, having friendships, developing skills, critically appreciating art, are not separate from the lives of persons. Unless life pervades these activities, they lack reality. They perfect the self, but the self they perfect is a bodily self that pervades them.

Third, one experiences oneself as a unity, not as an aggregate of entities organized into a system. This experience pervades our awareness of purposeful human acts. Such acts are integrated "doings" of a unified, living being. They are not experienced as the directing of instrumentalities by self-consciousness.

Joseph Boyle and Germain Grisez make a related point, observing:

> In general, the constituting of oneself through one's human acts is a realization of the potentialities which belong to and are characteristic of one's given self. The given self is oneself; its flourishing in activity is not a different thing from the unfolding of oneself. If the person as already given, as a basis for morally significant acts, were something distinct from the person as end, then this conception of human activity would be false. What, then, would unite these two principles? Are we to say that there is a third something—the real self—which unites the given self with the person? This proposal only complicates matters, for now it is necessary to ask what this third something has to do with the other two, how it united them while remaining distinct from them, and so on.[21]

Finally, and most compelling, I would offer an argument reductio ad absurdum against dualism. If one's reflections on the question of personhood begin from one's awareness of oneself as a unitary being, all the distinctions that one can draw among aspects of one's self in the course of one's reflections will be distinctions within one's experienced unity. Dualism is a theory that divides the unitary being of the person into distinct realities, thus running contrary to the starting point of one's reflections. So the dualist will not be able to say whether the "I" who is doing the reflecting and engaging in philosophical discussion is the non-bodily-person who inhabits a body or the mere-living-body it inhabits. If one identifies the "I" with the non-bodily-person, the living organism experienced by oneself and recognized by others as the reality whose behavior constitutes philosophical thought and communication is detached from the person doing the thinking and talking or writing. And if the "I" is identified instead with the mere-living-body, whose behavior does indeed communicate thoughts, the non-bodily-person is detached from the only reality recognizable as the person communicating. "Non-bodily-person" and "mere-living-body" are, we should conclude, constructs, neither of which pick out the dynamic, complex, but unified self who originally set out to explain its own reality.

If dualism is, as I have argued, an untenable position, traditional morality is correct, at least insofar as it affirms that bodily life is an intrinsic aspect of human persons. Though life is not the *only* such aspect—not the *only* ultimate intelligible reason for action—life is *an* intrinsic human good, *an* ultimate intelligible reason for action.

That the life of a person in an irreversible coma, the life of someone capable of participating in no good other than the good of bodily life itself, is a very deprived and inadequate life should not lead us to conclude that the comatose individual is not (or is no longer) a person. Nor should we conclude that the human life instantiated in such a person is not a good. The motivational power of any good is enhanced by the prospect of a life enriched by many other goods. The prospect of being left with any one good, while deprived of all others, is hardly an emotionally appealing one. Still, *emotionally* appealing or not, the value of a human life, even in a permanently comatose person, has a *rational* foundation: if dualism is false, bodily life is a not merely instrumental reason for action. As such it is a reason to provide medical care just as one provides food and water.

NOTES

1. Daniel Callahan, *Setting Limits: Medical Goals in an Aging Society* (New York: Simon and Schuster, 1987), 53.

2. For a full explanation of this conception of free choice, and a cogent defense of free choice thus conceived, see Joseph M. Boyle, Jr., Germain Grisez, and Olaf Tollefsen, *Free Choice: A Self-Referential Argument* (Notre Dame, Ind.: University of Notre Dame Press, 1976). In the limiting case, one could freely choose to act on a subrational (e.g., emotional) motive in opposition to reason(s).

3. See especially Germain Grisez, "Against Consequentialism," *American Journal of Jurisprudence* 23 (1978): 21–72; John Finnis, *Fundamentals of Ethics* (Oxford: Oxford University Press, 1983), 86–93; John Finnis, Germain Grisez, and Joseph M. Boyle, Jr., *Nuclear Deterrence, Morality and Realism* (Oxford: Clarendon Press, 1987), ch. 9; and Joseph Raz, *The Morality of Freedom* (Oxford: Clarendon Press, 1986), part IV, especially ch. 13. For a legal philosopher's attempt to rebut the incommensurability thesis, see Michael Perry, "Some Notes on Absolutism, Consequentialism, and Incommensurability," *Northwestern University Law Review* 79 (1985): 967–82. For a reply to Perry, see Robert P. George, "Human Flourishing as a Criterion of Morality: A Critique of Perry's Naturalism," *Tulane Law Review* 63 (1989): 1455–74.

4. Callahan is emphatic that *only* in such a society would his proposal be valid. He maintains that until our own society more closely approximates the ideal he sketches, it should not adopt an age-based standard. See *Setting Limits,* 197–98.

5. Ibid., 54.

6. Ibid., 187.

7. Ibid., 193.

8. Ibid., 173.

9. Ibid., 194.

10. Ibid., 116.

11. Ibid., 65.

12. Ibid., 69, 71, 72.

13. Ibid., 75, 76.

14. Ibid., 76.

15. Ibid., 18.

16. Joseph Fletcher, "New Definitions of Death," *Prism* 2 (Jan. 1974): 14.

17. Callahan, *Setting Limits,* 169.

18. Ibid., 179.

19. Ibid., 182–83.

20. Ibid., 81.

21. Germain Grisez and Joseph M. Boyle, Jr., *Life and Death with Liberty and Justice* (Notre Dame, Ind.: University of Notre Dame Press, 1979), 378.

PART TWO

Legal and Jurisprudential Aspects of Age-Based Rationing

3

When Bungling Practice Is Joined to Absurd Theory: Doctors, Philosophers, and the Right to Die

HADLEY V. ARKES

During the famous debates between Abraham Lincoln and Stephen Douglas, Lincoln was moved to make a point that he did not care whether slavery was voted up or down in the separate territories, as long as the decision was made in a democratic way, with the vote of a majority. Lincoln pointed out that one could express indifference in this way only if one were dealing with a morally indifferent thing: Douglas was "perfectly logical," he remarked, in saying that any community that wants slaves has a right to have them—"if there is nothing wrong in the institution; but if you admit that slavery is wrong, he cannot logically say that anybody has a right to do a wrong."[1]

Years earlier, one of our founders, James Wilson, denied that we ever had a "right to do a wrong," even in the state of Nature. William Blackstone had written, in Book 1 of his *Commentaries,* that "the law, which restraints a man from doing mischief to his fellow citizens, though it diminishes the natural, increases the civil liberty of mankind."[2] To that observation, Wilson responded with a pointed, rhetorical question: "Is it part of natural liberty," he asked, "to do mischief to anyone?"[3] Even before the advent of civil society, we did not have a right to carry out an unjustified assault, to rape, to maim. And therefore, when civil society restrained our freedom to assault, rape, or maim, the law deprived us of nothing we ever had a right to do. In this manner, Wilson sought to show that we gave up no rights when we formed the Constitution or entered civil society; the purpose of the Constitution was not to create rights but to secure and enlarge the rights we already possessed by nature.[4] Again, we have, with Lincoln and Wilson, a reflection of the axiom of moral reasoning that was first expressed by Thomas Aquinas: that we cannot coherently claim a right to do a wrong.

Now, generations later—well past Wilson and Lincoln—we find academic philosophers offering precious, mischievous essays, trying to claim, in the interests of "privacy," that we have a "right to do a wrong." But the claim of a right to do a wrong comes into play only when someone is suffering resistance—someone else is interfering with our freedom to do as we like (perhaps our freedom to torture animals in the privacy of our homes). The claim of a right is made to fend off that resistance: to say that we have a right to have our freedom respected is to say that anyone who interferes with us is doing a "wrong"; and by a wrong we mean something they ought not do, something they are not justified in doing, even if it suits their interests or their pleasure. But, of course, the apt response on the part of the intervenors is that they too have "a right to do a wrong."

The claim cannot escape its incoherence, and anyone who spends much time among students will know that this is not the only example of incoherent "rights claims." "I have a right to believe that I don't exist." Who is the bearer of that right—the one who does not exist? In the age of Lincoln and Wilson these points did not have to be made among the literate. But in the age of Oliver Wendell Holmes and Harry Blackmun, it does become necessary to remind even jurists and some doctors of law that rights cannot be created merely through stipulation. In October 1988 at a conference on euthanasia at Clark University, a group of us were encouraged to reflect again on a classic statement for euthanasia, written in the 1920s by Herr Doktor Professor Karl Binding. His essay bore the title, "Permitting the Destruction of Unworthy Life." I would not say that Binding argued, it would be more apt to say that he asserted the freedom to take one's own life, and then, in a burlesque move, he suggested that "natural law" itself would provide grounds for calling this freedom the primary human right.

In other words, we are asked to accept as a postulate of our freedom or autonomy that our identity as rights-bearing persons begins with our freedom to take our own lives. This construction was not all that distant from current fashions in moral philosophy, in which we see writers simply positing a basic claim to autonomy as the attribute of a moral agent—and then drawing from that premise of autonomy the right to do to oneself virtually anything one wishes to do in the name of that personal autonomy. In this way, writers seem to suffer no strain simply in asserting a "right to die," or a "right to take one's own life," as though the statements had an axiomatic quality—as though they merely had to be stated in order to establish their own validity. But that rendition removes the notion of autonomy from its moral foundations—the only foundations that provide its coherence and rationale as a moral postulate.

I recall, in this respect, a notable doctor from Los Angeles, who attended the conference at Clark. In a private conversation, he challenged my argument by posing the problem to me of one of his patients, a woman in her twenties who was paraplegic and quite depressed. She had come to the melancholy judgment that she simply did not wish to go on with her life. As the doctor pointed out, she was free to take her life; she had the means to do it—and therefore how could we deny that she had the right to take her life? Now to say that she was free to take her life is simply to say that she had the means, and that we may not be able, practicably, to prevent her from committing suicide. But, of course, even people who reflect only dimly on moral matters will usually understand that a statement of capabilities does not supply a statement of moral justification. I may be free to take the life of my neighbor, in the sense that I have the means of doing it, but this report on the state of my capabilities could not possibly establish that I would be *justified* in taking the life of my neighbor. To say that I *can* kill Jones is patently different from saying that I would be morally right or justified in killing Jones. That much would be evident to any child new to moral reasoning. But it should be equally evident that my capacity to take my own life could not establish that I have a right to take my life, or a right to die. The question then is: what needs to be added to the sentence? Or, what do we need to establish as the ground of our judgment before we could be warranted in drawing the conclusion that I would be *justified* in killing Jones or that I would have a *right* to kill myself? The answer, simply put, is that we would have to explain what is *rightful* or *justified* about these acts. But that is to say that we would have to go back to the ground of logic that would have to underlie any statements we could make about the things that are rightful or wrongful.

Immanuel Kant once made clear that the idea of autonomy was indeed central to the notion of a moral agent who had the freedom to choose his own course, to will his own acts. The language of morality—the language of praise and blame—made sense only in the domain of freedom, for actors who were animated by intention and will. The language of morality made no sense in relation to the domain of determinism, where events were determined by the laws of physics. If Smith is thrown out of a window and, on the way down, lands on Jones, we do not hold Smith responsible for an assault.

The language of morality applies only to the domain of freedom, but not all free, animate beings are moral agents. Animals may be free, but they cannot claim the standing of moral agents because they do not have access to the moral understanding that could govern their acts of choice. That may be why even today in the era of the rights of animals, we hear no insistence that we obtain the informed consent of dogs and cats to weigh the reasons or consider the justification for the surgery. In that respect, we do not recognize any claims to autonomy on the part of animals. We respect the claims of autonomy only in creatures who are able to deliberate on the question of whether the choices they make are good or bad, right or wrong, just or unjust. I reminded the doctor from Los Angeles that we are inclined to consider the opinions of his patient—to give them our respect-ful attention—precisely because we assume that we are dealing with a moral agent. But at the same time, we come to this paradox: the right to autonomy, the freedom to make a choice, is a right that arises only for a moral being. But it is the nature of a moral being that she is capable of reflecting about the moral ground of her choice: she can make judgments about the things that are right or wrong, and therefore *she can understand the things she is not free to choose in the name of her own autonomy.*

This understanding—so strange to our ears today—was far easier to grasp when it was understood that the moral laws were simply part of the laws of reason. To take the most elementary example, let us suppose we have a judge who says, "Farnsworth, you have been acquitted; therefore I sentence you to 20 years." The judge was in the domain of freedom, he had a judgment to make, and he made a mistake. We know he made a mistake because he violated the law of contradiction. He cannot say that Farnsworth was found innocent—not deserving of punishment—and then assign to him a heavy sentence. A harm is inflicted here by an agent in the domain of freedom (the judge); the harm is inflicted wrongly; and we know the act is wrong because it violated a law of reason, the law of contradiction.

Now let us suppose the judge said, "Farnsworth, you have been acquitted; therefore I sentence *myself* to 20 years." The nature of the wrong is not altered in any degree by the fact that the judge inflicts the punishment on himself. If we had the space here, I could show that any proposition that stands as a moral principle would find its ground, in the same way, in the laws of reason. I could defend that claim, for example, about the proposi-tion that people should not be held blameworthy for acts they were powerless to affect, or that it is wrong to assign benefits and disabilities to persons on the basis of race. And so, in a familiar problem, if we found a racist who was willing to kill people who were black, the wrongness of his act is not effaced in any way if he discovers that he himself had a black ancestor and is prepared to kill himself for the same, unjustified reason.

If the racist were suddenly affected by philosophic pretension, if he announced that he was invoking now his claim of personal autonomy to kill himself on account of the race of his ancestors, I hope it would be clear that this would remain an utterly incoherent claim of rights, a thoroughly invalid claim of personal autonomy, even though the killing was carried out solely against himself. And if we were faced with a patient citing this reason, invoking his claim to die, I hope we should not be standing there credulous—neither doctors nor lawyers nor judges—prepared to treat any such claim with even a trace of plausibility.

Again, it makes a notable difference to recognize that the ultimate grounds of these judgments are the canons of logic, the laws of reason. It is simply incoherent for anyone to claim that he has a "right to believe" that he does not exist; therefore, the proposition cannot supply a ground of justification for anything—neither for the killing of others nor the killing of one's self. That is to say, the logical incoherence of the proposition must be indifferent to the question of whether the killing is visited upon others or upon one's self. But in the same way we would come to discover many other, spurious grounds for suicide. They are spurious because they would seek to justify the taking of life by citing conditions or reasons that simply cannot establish a ground of right and wrong. We would readily recognize this fallacy at work if we claimed, say, the right to discontinue medical treatment for patients who were too tall or too short, with red hair or brown. We would find ourselves saying that these features were morally irrelevant: knowing the height or hair color of a man, we know nothing of his moral deserts—whether he is a good man or a bad man, whether he deserves punishment or reward, and whether he deserves to die.

The same point in principle can be made in relation to physical infirmities. I once gave my students the problem of a celebrated conductor who loses his hearing and concludes that a life without music is not, for him, a life worth living. But my students quickly came to understand that nothing in his deafness was the mark of wrongdoing, nor would this infirmity disarm him from leading a moral and creditable life. It could not be claimed, then, in any strictness, that a life of deafness was bound to be a useless or unsatisfying life if it were a life that still retained the possibilities for acting morally, acting sensitively, acting for good ends. My students recognized that it would be wrong to take the life of any other person because of his deafness, and, therefore, it would be quite as wrong to destroy one's own life for the same, indefensible reason.

But if that is the case, then I submit that the next step follows: if we do not have the right to do a wrong, even in the name of our personal autonomy—if we do not have a right of privacy that permits us to destroy ourselves when we are deaf—then it follows that we cannot delegate to other people a right of "substituted judgment" and permit them to order, in the name of our autonomy, a withdrawal of treatment that we would not be warranted in ordering, even for ourselves.

Now I trust it would be clear that this point of principle is quite indifferent to the malady or infirmity that patients are suffering. Do we think that people generally lose their claim to live when they lose their sight or their speech, when they suffer pain, or when they fall into a prolonged sleep? In none of these cases would we cite any condition of moral relevance, which could establish why anyone might deserve to die.

In none of these cases can people be justified in taking the lives of persons who are not their relatives because they suffer these infirmities. If that is the case, neither can they claim the right to do in their own relatives for these reasons. And if they cannot claim that authority, it is because the individual himself cannot claim the authority, because the individual himself cannot claim the license to take his own life—and make other people accomplices in the taking of his life—for reasons that cannot be justified.

When I offered these remarks at the Law School at the University of Illinois in October 1989, a member of the audience, a nurse from the state of Washington, came up to say that this account finally illuminated for her a vexing problem she had been encountering. She had been ministering to patients afflicted with AIDS. But some of those patients were demanding a right, in the name of their privacy, to withdraw from the medical treatment that might prolong their lives in a comatose state. What finally fell into place for the nurse was this chain of propositions. In order to justify the removal of medical care from a living patient with AIDS, one would have to explain, in effect, that something about the condition of AIDS made it justified or right to end the life of a patient. With the logic of moral justification, what made it right to remove medical aid from a patient with AIDS made it universally or impersonally right: it was a rightful thing that might be ordered *for* anyone in this situation, *by* anyone with the legitimate authority to decide. Through these steps, a personal decision is transformed into a doctrine or a license that may be employed now by people other than the patient: by relatives, perhaps, or even by administrators in a hospital, when the patient could not make decisions for himself. For after all, the administrators would now have been taught, as a point of doctrine, that patients with AIDS may be allowed to die rightfully. If a choice had to be made in the assignment of facilities, who could blame administrators if they assigned a lesser priority to patients who had sought to establish, as a matter of right, that they bore a condition that made it rightful to end their lives.

In his remarkable essay on "Destruction of Unworthy Life," Professor Binding had many stinging things to say about infirm people leading "absolutely valueless lives"—people who should mercifully be "freed from themselves," and could be, were it not for the spirit of this "enervated age." With all of his Teutonic charm and delicacy, Binding managed to confuse charged language with a medical standard. In his disposition, as it turned out, he was in advance of his age: he anticipated the way that the medical profession itself would move, in our time, to absorb into the canons of medical judgment the standards of a popular philosophy mingled with social science.

And so we find decisions are being made today on ending the lives of patients, and those decisions often pivot on the willingness of doctors to pronounce their patients to be in a "vegetative" condition or wanting in a "cognitive and sapient state." These terms are invoked as though they had standing as medical terms, but the doctors who use them know they are not merely speaking words of description. They are not merely purporting to *describe* the condition of their patients; they are naming the supposed conditions that are taken as *justifications* for ending the lives of the patients. Here, the doctors have glided, with naive serenity, into a domain well beyond their competence: it is by no means clear why any of these affirmations justify ending the life of a patient; that is a leap in judgment that requires no small exertion of moral reasoning. That discipline of moral judgment simply cannot be evaded by the casual claim that these patients are no longer really alive, as a human lives. For the claim is patently false, and, in fact, there is a need to invoke these terms of "vegetative" conditions, or to speak of patients lacking in a "cognitive" state, only because the patient has been indecorous enough to remain alive. For what does it mean, after all, to say that a patient has fallen into a "vegetative" condition? Has the patient suffered a change in genus? Has he declined from the condition of a sick human and taken on the properties of a radish? Or does the patient remain an infirm, sick human being, who happens still—happens, perhaps, regrettably, to the doctors or his family, but happens, nevertheless—to remain alive?

But this casualness in the brandishing of medical terms becomes even more dramatic and embarrassing in the matter of "cognitive and sapient" states. I remarked at a conference a few years ago that doctors and judges did not seem to be in a "cognitive" state as to the meaning of cognition itself. When the matter is understood strictly, cognition involves more than perception; it requires an understanding of the *rules of thought.* In the famous experiment by Jean Piaget, children saw beads poured from a low flat container into a high thin beaker and thought there were more beads in the higher container. These children *perceived* the event, but they did not have cognition of it. They would not understand the event until they had grasped the law of identity, or the law of the conversion of matter, which let them understand instantly that the same substance is persisting through changes in containers. But along with this confusion came a serious confusion on the part of courts about the evidence that was sufficient to establish the absence of a cognitive state—and therefore the withdrawal of any obligation to keep the patient alive. In this confusion, remarkably, the doctors offered no help to the courts; in fact, for men of science they showed a surprising want of serious reflection, or faintly demanding reasoning, in assessing the evidence that would support such a momentous conclusion.

On this question of the evidence, Professor Daniel Robinson has offered

the most telling commentary. Robinson recalled the experiment in which a
dog was conditioned to withdraw its limb at the sound of a tone. (The
sound of the tone was accompanied by a gentle shock, with the application
of a flame to the limb.) The dog may be paralyzed for a while with a drug
that makes movement impossible, even while it has no effect on the sensory
and perceptual capacities of the animal. In the state the dog is subject to a
regimen of conditioning in which the sound of the tone is no longer
followed by an aversive shock. When the drug wears off, the animal has
learned not to remove its paw at the sound of the tone. In other words,
learning has taken place even while the dog has been incapable of manifesting
any movement or showing any signs of alertness. As Robinson summed up
the matter, the absence of movement or signs of wakefulness could not be a
"sufficient and necessary condition for the proof of 'cognitive' or 'sapient'
capacity."[5] In some of the cases we have seen, doctors and judges have not
even bothered to determine whether the patient was capable of blinking
her eyes in response to their questions. *But even where there is no response to
questioning,* the point is that we are still not justified in leaping to the
inference that the patient is in some nonhuman state, utterly wanting in
cognition or understanding.

In the recent case of Nancy Jobes in New Jersey, it was reported that she
was able to track people with her eyes as they moved about her room; that
she would smile in response to loving or humorous remarks; that her face
would show relaxation when she was spoken to or touched in a soothing
manner. One physician reported that on four or five occasions he had said,
"Nancy, pick up your head," and that, with only one exception, she obeyed.[6]
Still, the N.J. Supreme Court managed to sweep past these points of
evidence in its willingness to license the relatives of Mrs. Jobes to end her
life. Judge Garibaldi noted for the court that these reports on the
responsiveness of Mrs. Jobes were "inconsistent with the trial court's conclusion that Mrs. Jobes was in a persistent vegetative state." In a show of judicial
novelty, Garibaldi argued that "evidence" may be " 'clear and convincing'
despite the fact that it has been contradicted." These reports had come
from two doctors, who had visited the patient once for ninety minutes.
Other doctors had not seen the same reactions, and they were not sure they
had seen anything more than physiological reactions, unaffected by feel-
ings or intentions. And yet there was no mention of any rebuttal or denial
of the responses noted by Doctors Victor or Ropper—e.g., Mrs. Jobes's
ability to lift her head on her own when she was asked. Judge Garibaldi
curiously referred to these reports as "opinions." But surely it was not a
matter of opinion as to whether Mrs. Jobes lifted her head or acted in
response to requests. Those are facts, and if they are true—if the report is
accurate—those facts should have been sufficient to dispose of the issue.

Imagine for a moment that the patient had been a mathematician, that most of the doctors thought he was in a vegetative state, and that only one time, for a few minutes, he had opened his eyes, grabbed a pencil, and written down a few equations. It would not matter that he had not written down the equations in the presence of other doctors, nor would it matter that he had done it only once, for a few minutes. The evidence would be sufficient to establish that he was not in a vegetative state. Or at least there should be enough doubt on the matter that a profession devoted to the care of the sick would have reason to continue that care and not end the life of the patient. It may now be hard to believe that as recently as three years ago we were still debating the question of removing food and water from a patient who was wanting in a "cognitive and sapient" state. But now, in the space of only a couple of years, the courts have swept past that dubious standard of a "cognitive and sapient" state; the judges have moved rapidly from the implausible to the indefensible, without affecting much awareness that they are crossing thresholds worth mentioning.

And so, in December 1987, the Supreme Court in the state of Washington carried this new jurisprudence into another phase. With the decision on Barbara Grant, the court broke away from the test of comatose states and articulated a willingness to remove medical support from patients who were quite evidently not comatose or unconscious. Barbara Grant was twenty-two; she had been afflicted since childhood with Batten's disease, a degenerative disease of the central nervous system. By October 1985 her condition had declined to the point that she could do nothing for herself, and her mother sought permission to remove the systems of support if Barbara should suffer a cardiac or respiratory arrest or if she should lose her ability to swallow. The judge, in the first instance, rejected the petition; for as grave as Barbara Grant's condition was, she was evidently not in a comatose state, and there was no need yet for intrusive medical procedures. Barbara's mother conceded that Barbara had never pronounced on the question of extraordinary medical measures, but her mother was convinced that Barbara would reject such treatment because, as the court reported, "Barbara had shown a dislike for the medical staff," as well as for the medication she had received and the suction tubes that had been used on her.[7]

All of this might be true, but a patient who had been so emphatic in conveying her dislike of the medical staff could hardly be said to be unconscious or wanting in a cognitive state. And yet, on appeal, the court swept these considerations aside. Justice Callow insisted on referring to Barbara Grant as a patient in a vegetative state, though she was quite evidently conscious and emphatic in her opinions. But consciousness was no longer a decisive consideration. As Justice Callow tried to sum up the rule he was inventing, it came out in this way: that life-sustaining treatment should not be required when a "patient is in an advanced state of terminal and incurable illness and is suffering severe and permanent mental and physical deterioration."[8]

Now, perhaps we are living in an age of grievance, but almost all people I know in their middle years claim to be encountering a decline in their physical and mental powers that they are convinced is permanent. There are people afflicted with diabetes, or mental retardation, or other infirmities that are irreversible. And almost any combination of these infirmities, worsening to a point of crisis, may furnish ample grounds for the Callows of the world to conclude that the continued life of these people is but an artificial contrivance.

I think it may be a telling mark of our current situation that the decision of the New York Supreme Court in the case of Mrs. O'Connor in 1988 has been understood as a conservative decision. There was an outraged dissent when the majority refused to allow food and water to be withdrawn from a seventy-seven-year-old woman at the request of her daughters. Mrs. O'Connor had suffered a series of strokes, but she was reported as "awake and conscious. She can feel pain, responds to simple commands, can carry on limited conversations, and is not experiencing pain." The majority showed a properly critical attitude toward the claims here, but they seemed to rest their judgment toward the point that Mrs. O'Connor had not really expressed her views clearly and emphatically on the question of sustaining her life. As Chief Judge Wachtler said, "No one should be denied essential medical care unless the evidence clearly and convincingly shows that the patient intended to decline the treatment under some particular circumstances."[9]

But it seems to be taken as plausible that if she *had* expressed herself precisely on this point, the court would have been willing to honor, as a legitimate project, the withdrawal of food and water from a patient who was quite unmistakably conscious and responsive. If Mrs. O'Connor had been unequivocal in announcing that she did not wish to live if the Mets did not survive the play-offs, I can hardly believe the courts would have taken the precision of her declaration as an adequate justification for the removal of food and water. But implicitly, the court would have accepted the decision in the case; and so once again, what the court passes over, as a settled assumption, may be far more revealing as a measure of our law and the current sensibilities of the judges.

The O'Connor case has been cited most recently by Chief Justice William Rehnquist in his opinion for the court in the case of Nancy Cruzan.[10] The chief justice strained to write a careful opinion, but the mischief of this case inheres precisely in the fact that the court has created the kind of license of suicide that was finally offered by Judge Wachtler in the O'Connor case. Or nearly: it is evident from the composition of Justice Rehnquist's opinion that he expended most of his effort in the case in trying to avoid that result. The case was billed as a test of the "right to die," and yet Rehnquist spent most of his decision evading the sweeping logic of a "constitutional right." Persistently, he preferred to describe the interest of the patient as a "liberty interest"[11]: it was rather like the "liberty to marry" or even the liberty to "walk down the street." Any person would have a legitimate interest in claiming these liberties in any of their innocent uses. But at the same time there is a recognition that not all uses of these liberties are innocent or harmless, and for that reason they may be restricted by the law at many plausible points. Our "liberty to walk down the street" may be restricted, with justification, when a fire department closes off a street to traffic while one of its units puts out a fire. Often these liberties may be puffed and described falsely as rights, as in the right to marry. But the court has made it clear that the so-called fundamental right to marry could not preclude a host of restrictions imposed by law: restrictions that confine marriage of two people, of different sexes, of the same species, of mature age, who are not related to one another already as fathers and daughters, mothers and sons. We may dignify the freedom engaged here with the label of a right, but the right in these instances could not be a categorical claim that trumps or overrides any attempt on the part of the law to impose restrictions.

Justice Rehnquist suffered no strain then in declaring that a "competent person has a constitutionally protected liberty interest in refusing unwanted medical treatment." But no sooner did he articulate that "interest" than he offered, in support, the precedents that exemplified the rightness of limiting that liberty. And so the first case he cited in support of this liberty was *Jacobson v. Massachusetts,* the classic case from 1905 that denied the right of a person to refuse a vaccine for smallpox.[12] Through most of his opinion Justice Rehnquist would not speak of a "right to die," but of the liberty of a patient—long recognized in the common law—to consent to his own surgery. And as Justice Anthony Scalia made clear in his concurring opinion, that ancient right of consent was never thought to confer a license on the part of the patient to commit suicide. Nor could it entail an obligation on the part of hospitals and doctors to act as accomplices. In other words, the traditional right to consent to surgery was never meant to suggest that a patient had a right to die or to take his own life for just any reason that may seduce his judgment. That liberty to decline surgery was thought to be quite consistent with the commitment of the common law to protect life and bar suicide.[13]

If the opinions written by Rehnquist and Scalia were taken together, they might offer a legal understanding quite consistent with the argument I have put forth in this essay. But in the opinion of the Supreme Court, the chief justice did not bring to the point of an explicit recognition the grounds on which the law may properly call into question the rightness, or the justification, of a patient to refuse medical treatment. For the sake, perhaps, of luring a fifth vote for a majority, the chief justice was willing to offer, in passing, this formula, which was not strenuously consistent with the cast of his opinion: Justice Rehnquist declared that, "for the purposes of this case, we assume that the United States Constitution would grant a competent person a constitutionally protected right to refuse lifesaving nutrition and hydration."[14] As the chief justice left the matter here, the doctrine he had produced was quite open to the man who would deny himself food and water because he discovered the existence of a black ancestor, or because he was suddenly afflicted with deafness, or because he did not wish to live if the Mets lost the play-offs. Of course, nothing in Justice Rehnquist's opinion bars judges and legislators from completing the moral project: it is still possible to fill in the standards of judgment, to remind the public that there are frivolous reasons for the taking of life—reasons that the law would not be obliged to honor, even when they are offered up by a patient in disposing of his own life.

What could be said for Justice Rehnquist is that he did nothing to prevent a serious effort of this kind: the law he fashioned could still be annexed to those moral requirements that must be respected by a patient, even when he claims to exercise his own autonomy and issue orders on his own medical treatment. But it must be said quite soberly, on the other side, that the chief justice did nothing to instruct doctors, patients, or judges about the principles that ought to guide their judgments. Set against the temper of our jurisprudence, that absence of teaching may be decisive: for those steeped in the premises of our current law, the absence of any teaching may merely confirm the assumption, comfortably settled, that there is nothing to be taught, that the mission of the law is to spin out ever more elaborate claims of rights, drawn from a notion of autonomy and personhood, but with no moral foundation to establish just why they are good, and just why they are justified.

I am not the first to suggest that the jurists of our own day suffer an embarrassment when they are measured against the first generation of jurists in this country. The judges of our own day are far less tutored in the traditional canons of philosophy and jurisprudence; they are simply more credulous and less resistant to the rationales served up to them under the authority of medical science. They could be helped immeasurably if doctors could preserve a more demanding sense of the kinds of evidence and measures that would be required in an authentic medical judgment. But when doctors play at philosophy, they become a band of affable utilitarians, winging it, hardly distinguishable any longer from judges, accountants, or anyone else these days who is inspired to say something philosophic.

Edmund Burke once remarked on the deranged political men who were trying to reshape the life of France according to the maxims of the French revolution. They were counting, he said, on "bumbling practice [to correct] absurd theory."[15] In our recent jurisprudence on euthanasia, we seem to find a medical profession permitting its practice to become bungling and vaudevillian as it is reshaped by moral sensibility that is skewed and a moral theory that must be regarded as sophomoric. The late Alexander King once offered some choice words about doctors who "deserved to die of their own specialty." My own prayer for the profession is that one day soon some of our doctors may be faced, not with a family claiming to vindicate the right of their uncle to die, but with a litigant claiming to act as a guardian for the patient—and to vindicate the right of the patient not to have his life ended by doctors joined to the service of bungling philosophy.

NOTES

1. *The Collected Works of Abraham Lincoln,* ed. Roy P. Basler (New Brunswick, N.J.: Rutgers University Press, 1953), 3:256–57.

2. William Blackstone, *Commentaries on the Laws of England* (Chicago: University of Chicago Press, 1979; orig. publ. 1765), vol. 1, book 1, 121–22.

3. James Wilson, "Of the Natural Rights of Individuals," in *The Works of James Wilson* (Cambridge, Mass.: Harvard University Press, 1967), 2:585–610, 587.

4. Ibid., 585. This understanding was woven into the arguments of the Federalists as they raised a serious concern about the logic of a Bill of Rights. For a fuller statement of this argument, see my chapter, "On the Dangers of a Bill of Rights: Restating the Federalist Argument," in Hadley V. Arkes, *Beyond the Constitution* (Princeton, N.J.: Princeton University Press, 1990), ch. 4.

5. Daniel N. Robinson, introduction, in *In the Matter of Karen Quinlan* (Lanham, Md.: University Press of America, 1976), vii, xi.

6. *In the Matter of Jobes,* 529 A.2d 434 (N.J. 1987). In the more recent case of Nancy Cruzan in Missouri, the attending nurses provided comparable points of testimony to contest the claim that Ms. Cruzan was in a comatose or vegetative state. These points were summarized in the briefs: "In 1988, Nancy Cruzan cried after a Valentine's Day card sent by her nieces was read to her by her nurse. . . . She has 'jumped' when scared by loud noise. . . . ('Nancy about came out of the bed.') She has cried after family visits. . . . When her nurses joked with each other about their relative professional skills, she 'snickered' and . . . thought she was about to laugh—when the nurse told her a funny story about the nurse's children and a skunk." Recalled by Robert Cynkar in his *amicus curiae* brief for the Knights of Columbus, 2.

7. *In re Grant,* 747 at 2d 445, at 448.

8. Ibid. at 453. In the immediate aftermath of the decision in *Grant,* the court

was "corrected" by the assistant attorney general on the current laws in Washington covering the withdrawal of medical care. Apparently the judges had not fully understood that under the current statutes the decision to withhold care from an incompetent patient did not require the consent of all the members of the family. As the judges moved to reconsider their order in the case, one member—Justice Dunham—decided to switch from the side of the majority. He joined a separate concurring and dissenting opinion written by Justice Anderson. Anderson had agreed with the majority on the right of Barbara Grant's family to remove medical treatment, but he rejected the notion that hydration and nutrition could be classified as a medical treatment. Two justices, Goodloe and Dore, dissented emphatically from the claim that anyone but a competent adult can make the decision to remove life-sustaining treatment from him/herself. The curious result, rendered in a box score, was a vote of 4-3-2. The defection of Justice Dunham had withdrawn the authoritative standing of a majority from the doctrine articulated by Justice Callow—the doctrine characterized by Justice Anderson as "unadorned euthanasia." But the practical effect, nevertheless, was to leave intact the decision in favor of Judith Grant, sustaining her right to remove medical treatment from her daughter. And so the switch of judges had nothing to brake the court from the movement to euthanasia marked so sharply by Callow's opinion. For the subsequent developments in this case, see Stephen P. VanDerhoef, *"In re Grant,"* *University of Puget Sound Law Review* 197 (1989). The "modified" version of *In re Grant* may be found at 757 at 2d 534 (1988).

9. *In re Westchester County Medical Center on Behalf of O'Connor,* 72 N.Y. 2d 517, 531 N.E. 2d 607 (1988).

10. *Cruzan v. Director, Missouri Department of Health* (1988).

11. Ibid., 13 and 14 of the slip opinion.

12. See 197 U.S. 11.

13. See Scalia, in the slip opinion, especially 3, 6–8.

14. Page 15 of the slip opinion.

15. Edmund Burke, "Letter to a Member of the National Assembly" (1791).

4

Target—The Elderly:
A Nondiscrimination Perspective
on Daniel Callahan's *Setting Limits*

ROBERT A. DESTRO

It is a truism that all arguments must begin somewhere, preferably at a point that would be identified by those engaged in them as "the beginning." Daniel Callahan's discussion of limiting health care for the elderly, *Setting Limits: Medical Goals in an Aging Society,*[1] is a good example of a timely and useful argument that begins somewhere other than where it should.

On the surface, *Setting Limits* is an argument for the development of an ethic governing law and medicine in a society in which the elderly are valued members of the community. It presents a case for encouraging physicians and their patients to have a clear sense of justice and proportion in the midst of life's terminal crises. It envisions a government committed to a transcendent vision of the common good and imagines a cadre of health-care bureaucrats who will not take intellectual or practical shortcuts in their well-meaning attempts to get their jobs done on time and (most importantly) under budget.

To a reader who is reasonably well informed about the medical, legal, and social ramifications of limiting access to health care, *Setting Limits* is intriguing and frustrating. It is intriguing because Callahan's recommendations represent a serious attempt to grapple with one of the most difficult bioethical and legal dilemmas facing our society. It is frustrating because the ideal world Callahan proposes as the goal of his argument will never come into being if policy-makers and families adopt Callahan's operative assumptions as their own. The reasons are as stark as they are simple.

In the real world Callahan describes, social value and the common good are too often measured in starkly political terms.[2] "Little thought is given in medicine to its ultimate ends" because physicians and patients, and the government upon which both rely to subsidize them, are more often captivated by technological possibilities than by any vision of the just and compassionate in the face of individual mortality. We live in a society "which in its secular and public guise professes to have no generally binding moral traditions,"[3] and in which attempts to construct a legal order based in transcendent notions of truth, justice or morality are likely to be challenged as unconstitutional "contradict[ions of] the 'logic of secular [individual] liberty' " that guides the current majority of the U.S. Supreme Court.[4]

Callahan recognizes all of this; that is why *Setting Limits* is, ultimately, an open invitation for discussion. The book sketches out an approach—the author calls it a "trajectory"[5]—that he hopes will lead unerringly toward the targeted goal: an enlightened social policy toward the elderly and the dying.

"Trajectory" is an apt term for Callahan's approach—more so, I believe, than he intended. He has launched an idea and set it hurtling toward an elusive target called "intergenerational equity." Its inherent concept and design flaws will assure that it will never reach that goal.

Callahan acknowledges that weaving an integrated social tapestry requires collective effort and a common set of values.[6] He eloquently describes (and decries) the existing values that seem to govern medical-care decision-making and accurately views them as one source of our inability to come to grips with the moral limits of health-care decisions. Finally, he makes his own suggestions regarding an alternative set of values that should guide individuals in making judgments about the limits of medical care. For all of this he is to be commended, even if one does not agree either with his approach or his suggestions.

The problem is that while he decries the present value structure that influences medical-care decision-making, he makes no effort to demonstrate that his approach rests on values that are, in any meaningful way, different from those he rejects as the source of the problem: "the virtues of youth rather than age, the new rather than the old, self-reliance and autonomy rather than community."[7] The result is predictable.

Like a surface-to-surface missile with a misprogrammed inertial guidance system, his idea veers off its intended course as it starts downrange and targets the very individuals Callahan considers to be at risk: the elderly. Given his initial value judgments and assumptions,[8] it will be difficult, if not impossible as a practical matter, for society to attain the intergenerational equity he urges. An approach centered on the duties of the elderly alone[9] is more likely to result in an increasingly overt tendency to justify devaluation of and discrimination against the elderly and other persons with disabilities.

I make two basic arguments concerning the serious questions raised in *Setting Limits.* Both underscore the importance of reaching agreement on fundamentals before embarking on the always difficult task of formulating a set of social, medical, or legal policy goals. Callahan's quote from Michael Ignatieff's book, *The Needs of Strangers,* captures the point nicely: "woe betide any man who depends on the abstract humanity of another for his food and protection."[10] In my view, intergenerational equity as proposed in *Setting Limits* is a potentially dangerous abstraction unless and until it is complemented by a clearly articulated vision of the place and value of the elderly and disabled in the community at large.

The second argument is that the provision, financing, and rationing of medical services should be no less subject to scrutiny under the nondiscrimination laws than any other profit-making, nonprofit, or charitable activity.[11] I shall not quarrel with the fact that at the individual level medical decision-making affects important personal and familial interests. Nor shall I dispute the inability of law or constitutional principle to lay down fixed standards for the exercise of medical judgment. The argument here is that neither the personal nor the technical nature of medical decision-making exempts it from scrutiny intended to determine whether or not the criteria utilized for making health-care judgments are consistent with the ultimate goal of nondiscrimination law itself: to do justice and effectuate the common good.

Thankfully, however, my task here is limited. For present purposes, I shall leave a discussion of both the limits of autonomy and the substantive content of intergenerational justice to those more qualified than I to address such topics. My topic is nondiscrimination, and the intensely interesting question of how society sets, marks, and polices the boundaries between the exercise of legitimate judgment and the practice of illicit discrimination.

Fundamental Questions: Looking for the Starting Point

My first argument is that while *Setting Limits* raises many of the right philosophical and moral questions about medical and social goals in a just society, it analyzes them on the basis of a set of assumed principles that appear to be fundamentally at odds with the natural rights philosophy that undergirds both the civil order under which we live and Callahan's basic ethical argument about the necessity to accept nature's limits on the human lifespan. I propose to demonstrate why this is so by posing a series of questions.

Why the Elderly?

Perhaps the most basic question is why *Setting Limits* is about the elderly. Callahan answers that he wrote the book "because some significant change in our thinking about health care for the elderly is needed" and that he wanted to start a "long-term discussion" that would address the ancient question: how much is enough?[12]

But why the elderly? One can, and perhaps all of us should, ask the question "how much is enough?" far more often and in far more circumstances than we usually do, but why should the elderly be singled out for special consideration here?

If the question is "how much is enough?" it is equally relevant to ask it in the case of *any* patient, elderly or not, who has, based on Callahan's thesis about the ethical limits of health care, arguably "had enough." In his zeal to urge society to pay more attention to the question of intergenerational equity, Callahan has unjustifiably narrowed the appropriate scope of the question from "how much is enough?" to "how much is enough for an elderly person?"

The reasons for limiting the argument to the elderly appear to be fourfold: first, the geometric increase in the number of elderly persons; second, the virtual certainty that many, if not most, will suffer from either chronic illness or age-related disability (or both) prior to their deaths; third, the increasing isolation and loneliness of many elders; and fourth, that these developments already involve enormous human and social costs that will only increase with the passage of time.[13]

All of this is true. But it still begs the question "why the elderly?" It is absolutely critical to establish at the outset whether the problem is to be defined as the elderly themselves, their excessive demands for health care, or the generally excessive demand for health care brought about by this society's tendency to view "medicine . . . as a means of trying to cure or control the problems of life."[14]

If Callahan is correct that the elderly mirror commonly held societal perceptions about the role of medicine, Callahan's exclusive focus on the excessive demand for medical care by the elderly is difficult to justify. And if the goal of *Setting Limits* is to lay a foundation for discussion of the ends of health care, including equity and justice for all who seek medical care (including those who cannot afford it), Callahan's focus must be broadened to include a discussion of society's vision of justice and the common good. In short, the role of the elderly in attaining intergenerational equity is an important part of the inquiry, but reference to the obligations of others is necessary, too—unless, of course, we are to assume that the elderly themselves are the problem.

Callahan seems to want it both ways. Even though he strenuously argues that the elderly should not be devalued, his express arguments and the logic from which they are derived squarely target them for special treatment. A prime example is the suggestion that insulin be denied to elderly patients with "mild impairment of competence."[15] Since Callahan rightly decries the danger that excessive individualism and self-absorption pose in high-cost, high-technology medicine, there is something incongruous about this suggestion. Insulin therapy is neither high-cost nor high-technology medicine; it is routine therapy for a chronic condition that affects both children and adults.

The conclusion is inescapable: *Setting Limits* is not about excessive individualism and self-absorption, both of which lead inevitably to inequitable demands on the health-care system. The book is about dependent persons (primarily elderly), their place in community and family, "the meaning and significance of old age" in a society with an "absence of a public philosophy on the meaning of aging,"[16] and the problems dependent and disabled persons create in a society that values individualism, personal autonomy, youth, and vigor.

What Do We Owe the Elderly?

This is the central question of the book, for Callahan is certainly correct in noting that "if the elderly lack an established, coherent and meaningful place in life and society, there is no real rationale for their protection" in a secular society; "it merely exists as a kind of sentimental beneficence."[17] I agree that it is essential that this question be posed directly, free of the " 'evasion, disguise, temporizing [and] deception by which artfully chosen allocation methods can avoid the appearance of failing to reconcile values in conflict.' "[18] But even this formulation manages to evade the moral dilemma. Allocation methods are but one way to resolve the question. Another way is to focus on the elderly alone, without explicit regard for the manner in which such a focus will resonate in a culture he condemns.

To be sure, Callahan recognizes the "possibilities for moral mischief"[19] in both *Setting Limits* and in its recently published sequel, *What Kind of Life: The Limits of Medical Progress.* In the latter, he answers the question "why the elderly?" as follows: "In attempting to provide ever-improved health care for the elderly, we are on the greatest, and most extensive, of medicine's many frontiers of progress. [*Setting Limits*] was as much a study of how to respond to such a frontier as it was a book about the elderly. . . . It is quite true that it is our whole system that is in turmoil, not just our attempt to provide for those who are aged."[20]

What Kind of Life underscores the importance of an inquiry into the general nature and extent of social obligation to those with medical needs. If the aim of Callahan's overall project is "to set forth an alternative way of thinking about health that will lead into the devising of a reasonable and just health-care system[, . . . which is] deeply rooted in a plausible understanding of the human condition and . . . coherent, feasible, and humane in its practical policy implications," then the "trajectory" problems in *Setting*

Limits arise from its focus on the elderly and what they expect from others in the community.[21]

It makes no difference that "we begin [the discussion] in media res, in the middle of the story, with a hard, deeply ingrained set of values, a complex set of institutions, and a bewildering array of mores, folkways, interests, and predilections already in place [that] will not be easy to change."[22] As long as there is agreement on fundamentals (i.e., the ultimate starting point of the total inquiry), it makes no difference that a particular discussion starts in the middle: the goal will determine the range of possible trajectories. If the starting points are different—and they are—there can be no agreement on process until there is common ground for discussion.

Unlike Callahan, I do not believe that "we [as a society] lack good moral and cultural resources" to resolve these value questions.[23] The moral and cultural resources are as available now as they ever were.[24] The question is whether those in positions of authority and influence, like Callahan himself, have the insight and courage to draw upon those resources explicitly and to use them to examine "the possibilities for moral mischief" inherent in their own perspectives. Such an examination should be complete before any attempt is made to "reform" what are quite accurately described as a "bewildering array of mores, folkways, interests, and predilections already in place."

It is precisely because Callahan suggests a change in the terms of the debate that a brief review of one of the more important sources of the "mores, folkways, interests and predilections" in American society—civil rights law—is in order. The law is both a component and a reflection of the "moral and cultural resources" of a society. An examination of "the ethics of equal protection" highlights the essential soundness of Callahan's indictment of "an unlimited quest for individualistic pleasure" and underscores the danger of his narrowly targeted approach.

Age, Disability, and Civil Rights:
The Ethics of Equal Protection

Duty and Its Relevance to Civil Rights

Duty is not a topic that receives much attention in contemporary American civil rights discourse. From the beginning, the concept of equal protection of the laws was described by the U.S. Supreme Court as "a positive immunity or right," a claim particularly valuable to its intended beneficiaries, the newly freed slaves.[25] The debate over the character of the equal protection guarantee[26] rages in similar terms today,[27] with no apparent end in sight.[28]

The conceptual shortsightedness of a rights-based approach to equal protection has complicated many, if not most, discussions of issues such as affirmative action and the development of standards to govern discrimination on the basis of age and disability. The reason is simple: rights claims are assertions that collective interests are limited when they limit individual liberty and autonomy. The claims made by dependent persons on the community are qualitatively different. Thus, I begin this argument with a basic proposition: Duty, not right, is the organizing concept behind the constitutional guarantee of equal protection of the laws.

In most discussions relating to the nature of individual liberties, the central concern is whether the personal interest in question can be characterized as a matter of right, that is, shall the individual be at liberty to seek enjoyment of the claimed interest without governmental or private interference? Although the resolution of such claims involves an inevitable balancing and subordination of one set of interests to another, the sum total of governmental obligation is to refrain from acting in a manner that will deprive a person of the asserted right.[29] We therefore speak, quite correctly, in terms of a "right" to freedom of speech and a "right" to religious liberty.

The constitutional and legal guarantees of equal protection are different; they require more than simple restraint from interference in another's liberty; their function is to require that governments and individuals conform their behavior to a legally and socially acceptable standard.[30] The liberties of speaking or publishing freely can exist whether others listen or read.

Thus, while the goal of the constitutional guarantee of equal protection of the law is equal enjoyment of the blessings of liberty, its foundation is a behavioral obligation. To state that all persons are entitled to "equal protection of the laws" is to express a social duty on the part of government that has been codified as a matter of constitutional law.[31] Although the courts have generally rejected claims that liberty-based rights claims presuppose affirmative community obligations to support the full enjoyment of those liberties by anyone,[32] there is considerably more sympathy for such claims in the equal protection context,[33] especially where the claimants are in a condition of dependency.[34]

It is particularly relevant to note that American law has only recently added the elderly and persons with disabilities to those deemed to be at risk from the antisocial behavior of others. In part, this development is attributable to demographic change—an increase in the number, health, and mobility of elderly and disabled persons—due to the advances in health care addressed in *Setting Limits*. Equally important, however, is the gradual acceptance of the proposition that reason rather than prejudice must govern public policy affecting persons with disabilities.[35]

But precisely because accommodating an elder or a person with a disability requires more than merely a fair application of a set of neutral criteria, consensus concerning the nature and extent of affirmative community obligations remains fragile.[36]

What Duty—and to Whom?
Of Potential and Personhood

The basic question explored in *Setting Limits* is what is the extent of our duty—as a society and as individuals—to the elderly? Although expressed as a single question in most instances,[37] the structure of this question throughout Callahan's inquiry obscures the fact that this question has two parts: first, "what duty?" (the scope of the obligation); and second, "to whom is it owed?" (its object).[38] For this discussion, I will address the questions in reverse order.

To Whom Is the Duty Owed?   Although Callahan and I approach both the nature and scope of duty in the health-care setting quite differently, we agree that the basic issue is one of duty. Our first, and most important, difference lies in our respective views concerning the people who are the subject of *Setting Limits:* the objects of society's duty.

Callahan's approach combines the questions of object and scope into a lengthy discussion about specific circumstances in which society should reach agreement about the limits of health care. This has the effect of making the scope of even the most basic legal duty of the state—to protect each member of the community from harm—depend upon the characteristics of the person to be protected. I speak simply in terms of the duty of those in authority to offer all persons an equal, basic level of protection.[39]

Since the Constitution speaks in terms of a duty to provide protection to all persons on an equal basis, the source of our difference in perspective must be in our respective answers to the question: "who is a person?" Who are those members of the community to whom society collectively owes a duty to provide equal protection of the laws? Because *Setting Limits* is intended as an invitation for discussion of medical and social goals in a just society, the first clue that there is a programming error in Callahan's trajectory is apparent as soon as his answer to this question is examined.

Before doing so, however, it is important to note that Callahan and I do not disagree over the legitimacy of debating the standards under which decisions will be made concerning the extent and relative priority of duties alleged to be in conflict in any medical setting. Problems of priority and degree are implicit in virtually every ethical dilemma; medical and social ethics are no different.

Discussions of extent and priority of treatment in a medical setting presuppose the existence of more basic duties to the patient. Raising the question of personhood changes the nature of the discussion because it challenges the existence of even these basic duties. Where the subject of discussion is a person, the nature of the ethical, moral, and legal duty is qualitatively different from that in which the object of the duty is not.[40]

Callahan seeks to soften the significance of a discussion of personhood by stating in advance that "the crucial potentialities for personhood" present "a complex and controversial question."[41] Given that the question of personhood is another way of asking who shall be considered a member of the community, such a concession is more important for what it leaves unstated than for what it says (which is not much).

The implicit message is that there are indeed some individuals now considered to be members of the community who might be better thought of as outsiders (i.e., as dead people) for purposes of public policy. Thus, not only is the substantive question—who is a person?—"complex and controversial," but so is the implicit assumption that the community has the right to define any of its living members as outsiders. Callahan, however, simply assumes the appropriateness of both questions in the context of the discussion, states three potentialities he considers crucial, and proceeds to construct the entire argumentative edifice of *Setting Limits* around them.

From Callahan's perspective, membership in the community turns upon (1) the potential capacity to reason; (2) the potential to have emotions; and (3) the potential to enter into relationships with others. A person who has lost all these capacities cannot, in a way meaningful to Callahan, be called a "person" any longer, or be said to have a "biographical life" remaining.[42]

Cases once thought difficult, such as *In re Conroy,*[43] *Matter of Jobes,*[44] and *Cruzan v. Director, Missouri Department of Health,*[45] become easier through the magic of redefinition. An individual in a persistent vegetative state is no longer a person, but "a being." The nature of social duty changes because the object of that duty is no longer a member of the human community. The duty of protection that is owed a person in law and morality has vanished, and in its place exists only the duty to act with "the respect due human bodies prior to clinical death."[46]

That this is a "a complex and controversial" approach is obvious, but that commentators have not appeared to notice its importance is disturbing. Callahan suggests that individuals who are not dead under any of the relevant clinical criteria are to be treated as if they were dead. Members of the community who are nearly, but not quite, dead become "bodies" because they lack "the crucial potentialities for personhood."

Such a concept of personhood is far too narrow. It defines personhood in terms of "crucial potentialities" and makes the otherwise absolute duty of law and society to provide equal protection for individuals contingent on their natural ability.[47] Under Callahan's approach, only those without disabilities are assured equal legal protection from harm.

Keeping in mind that the object of the Fourteenth Amendment was to protect all who were, by their nature, human,[48] it is appropriate to examine Callahan's ability-based construct with a view toward determining whether it is consistent with his own argument that nature itself provides the most relevant criteria for decision-making (i.e., a natural lifespan). The inherent inconsistencies in Callahan's approach become clear when one examines not the comparative level of protection to be afforded the elderly (although that is instructive, too), but his treatment of the elderly themselves.

The Significance of Age: Disability and "Potential." Under Callahan's approach, society owes persons with disabilities very little. That which it does owe appears to be related to the type of disability and inversely proportional to the degree to which it affects the key potentialities. This much is clear from the trajectory elaborated throughout the book. But even in the case of the "physically vigorous elderly person," Callahan would support withholding care.[49]

Given his focus on potential and intergenerational equity, there is no theoretical problem for Callahan here: age itself is a disability in that the "natural" lifespan operates inexorably to limit the potential of elderly people. There is, however, a practical objection to operationalizing such a suggestion. Callahan "do[es] not think anyone would find it tolerable to allow a healthy [elderly] person to be denied lifesaving care.[50]

Quite so, and it is revealing that Callahan does not inquire as to the reasons for such "intolerance"; for he might just find evidence of the "moral and cultural resources" he alleges are lacking in contemporary society. My own suspicion is that society is morally and culturally unprepared at present either to write off those who "deteriorate" or become disabled, or to treat persons who are not dead as if they were.[51]

It is significant that, although it is the centerpiece of his entire argument about intergenerational equity, Callahan never defines the term "potential." This omission is important for several reasons. First, it converts inter-generational equity into a dangerous abstraction. Second, the duties such an equitable principle would impose seem to depend entirely on the undefined "potential" of the person whose contribution is expected. And third, the only real difference between persons with disabilities and the elderly are their respective ages. For both groups, life "potential" appears to be that which others are willing, given the nature and extent of their particular disability, to attribute to them; technologically assisted potential has already been ruled out.

This is the real significance of Callahan's three "crucial potentialities for personhood." The potential capacity to reason, to have emotions, and to enter into relationships with others cannot logically be limited to the elderly. In fact, the case for denying treatment to a young person without much potential for reason, emotion, and relationships would be even stronger under Callahan's logic than it would be for elderly patients with "mild impairment[s] of competence"[52] or to unborn children. Elderly patients with mild impairments of competence have actual (although limited) capacity to reason, they have some, if not all, of their natural capacity to experience emotions, and actual (although again perhaps limited) capacity to enter into relationships with others. Unborn children have immense capacity for all three,[53] assuming they are allowed to be born.

Nevertheless, Callahan suggests that the intergenerational equity proposed in *Setting Limits* requires that only the elderly should be denied treatment. Such equity would prefer the young patient with potential (perhaps a poet) who suffers, for example, from end-stage HIV infection (AIDS) in the allocation of medical resources. If this person should have access to expensive, high-technology medical treatment in an effort to prevent or retard the inexorable result of the disease because of an assumed potential, what then should be the societal response to another person with severe AIDS-related dementia? If there is to be a choice, on what basis will it be made? Age or potential? The answer to that question would have to be potential, however defined (probably politically). A grandmother who has diabetes and (arguably) no potential because she is old will get nothing, not even insulin. She loses on both counts, no matter how much actual potential she has remaining.

And thus we return to the starting point of this discussion: the ethics of the equal protection guarantee. If, as Richard John Neuhaus has said, our jurisprudence of civil rights holds that "human rights are coterminous with the individual's ability to claim and exercise such rights,"[54] the law is in a difficult position indeed. By its very terms the equal protection clause of the Fourteenth Amendment imposes a duty to provide protection regardless of one's capacity to demand it.

The conclusion is inescapable: despite Callahan's strenuous arguments and exhortations to the contrary, acceptance of his related concepts of a "natural" lifespan and a "tolerable death"[55] as a matter of public policy will inevitably result in the discrimination against and devaluation of the elderly he fears. Because both concepts proceed from implicit assumptions about the requisites of a "good life" and the potential one must have to be a person, they can also serve as the intellectual basis or justification for discrimination against persons of any age who have severe disabilities.

What Duty and How Much?
Of Nature and Extent

Nondiscrimination Generally.   The law governing discrimination on the basis of handicap, disability, and age is developing rapidly. Federal law requires that any federally funded program or activity must refrain from discriminating against an "otherwise handicapped" individual "solely on the basis of his handicap."[56] Many state and local laws provide similar protection. The newly enacted Americans with Disabilities Act[57] will effectively bring persons with disabilities under the full protection of the civil rights laws in employment, transportation, and public accommodations, including hospitals and health-care facilities.[58] The coverage of law governing discrimination on the basis of age is also expanding.[59] Without attempting a detailed analysis of current federal case law on the related, but distinct, topics of disability and age discrimination, it seems clear that the trend in enacted and decisional law governing both the elderly and persons with disabilities is to treat them with greater, not lesser, respect and concern.

These are welcome trends, for they reflect not only the law's increasing awareness that the number of elderly Americans is growing, but also an increasing societal affirmation of the natural rights ethic under which neither age nor disability should serve as a morally or socially adequate basis for denying equality before the law. The law correctly requires more narrowly tailored justifications for treating individuals as outsiders in their own community.

Age, Disability, and Capacity.   For the purposes of this essay, it is useful to consider discrimination on the basis of age and disability as related rather than separate categories. The central inquiry in both cases is twofold: individual capacity, and the extent of the duty to accommodate.

In a series of cases expanding on the meaning of federal laws governing the rights of persons with disabilities, the U.S. Supreme Court has pointed out that Congress was motivated by two concerns: to protect the handicapped from the intentionally discriminatory acts of others[60] and to eliminate what might be called "benign neglect" based on "thoughtlessness and indifference."[61]

Setting Limits, by contrast, is both thoughtful and thought-provoking. The standards Callahan proposes are active ones, although they will operate in a medical milieu in which "benign neglect" based on "thoughtlessness and indifference" remains all too common with respect to the treatment of persons with disabilities.[62] For practical purposes, this means that the exercise of discretion to deny treatment must be closely monitored.

Regulating Medical and Social Discretion in an Age of Limits.   We now reach my second argument: health-care decision-making, including the exercise of judgment by medical personnel, is not exempt from regulation in the public interest. Callahan agrees. Decisions to end life, whether voluntary or not, are not simply private matters. Society can and should demand medically and socially legitimate reasons for health-care decision-making.

On what basis are we to determine the extent of the duty to provide medical care? The answer is easily framed in the negative: the extent of duty must not depend solely on the patient's age or level of disability. This is not because the law forbids making judgments on these grounds—in fact, it all too often permits them[63]—but rather because neither age nor disability alone is a demonstrably legitimate standard for medical- or health-care decision-making by physicians or anyone else, especially government.

In my view, the selection of age or disability (i.e., potential) as the primary standard for allocating scarce medical resources is unjust. Because it is also unreasonable to take the position that the physical characteristics of patients are irrelevant to the medical-care decision-making process, the real question is: what weight should age and disability be given in that process? My answer is precisely the opposite of Callahan's.

Callahan correctly points out that there is a distinction between medical and moral decision-making. The problem, as he sees it, is that traditional medical-care decision-making treats age as a physical factor influencing technical judgment. His proposal is that it should be viewed as an appropriate moral factor as well.[64] Given that Callahan's argument is a moral one, this is a logical suggestion. Given its legal implications if accepted, it is appropriate to examine it in light of the legal duties governing professional service providers.

Since the nature of a relationship generally governs the legal and ethical duties that inhere in it, the focus here will be on the kind of relationship established between the decision-makers and the individual to whom they owe a professional duty. Lawyers, for example, have duties that are both technical and ethical and these arise both from the nature of their relationship with their clients and from their position as officers of the court.[65] The same can be said for parents and families: legal and moral duties arise from the nature of the familial or parental relationship. The duties of medical professionals have similar legal and moral roots.

When the law undertakes to scrutinize the legitimacy of professional behavior, the inquiry is necessarily broad: the action, decision, or proposal is to be viewed in the context of the professional relationship and community in which it takes place. The burden and allocation of proof in professional malpractice and civil rights cases proceeds in this fashion.

The purpose of *Setting Limits* is to suggest standards for the exercise of medical judgment.[66] That social consequences flow from medical judgments is a given, but at the basic decision-making level the first consideration is always technical: "can it be done?" Callahan's focus in *Setting Limits* is the ethically necessary second step of the decision-making process: "should it be done under the circumstances?" To this point, Callahan and I agree that "the problem [at this stage] is distinguishing between medical and moral judgment."[67] We differ from this point onward because Callahan fails to take his own advice.

The purpose of medical-care decision-making is medical, that is, to affect the physical or mental condition of individual patients, including the relief or palliation of pain. Whatever decision is made will have moral consequences as well, but the character of the decision remains medical. The question posed in *Setting Limits* is whether the moral issue will be addressed directly and, in Callahan's own words, free of the "evasion, disguise, temporizing [and] deception by which artfully chosen allocation methods can avoid the appearance of failing to reconcile values in conflict."[68] The conflict of values becomes apparent only after the question is first correctly identified as one of medical judgment. Only then are the important moral consequences seen in context.

This is where the trajectory sketched out in *Setting Limits* misses the mark. In his zeal to condemn the trend toward greater and greater individual freedom of choice in medical matters, Callahan entirely ignores the question of personal responsibility. Whether the decision is made at the individual or at the societal level through allocation of resources,[69] the decision-maker bears personal, moral responsibility for every decision. This means that whatever decision is made must be explained, and that the person or entity making the decision must be prepared not only to defend the explanation, but also to justify the source of his, her, or its competence to make it in the first place.

I would argue that civil rights law has already rejected Callahan's argument that doctors—or legislatures, for that matter—should be making moral judgments about the protection to be afforded entire classes of persons. The law requires that medical judgments, like other professional judgments, be made on the basis of medical rather than social criteria. Otherwise, there is no effective standard for review.

To the extent that age or disability is demonstrably relevant to medical decision-making, both are legitimate criteria for the exercise of medical judgment, both technical ("can it be done?") and ethical ("will it serve its intended purpose in these circumstances?"). The same is true respecting moral or social judgments concerning the relevance of age and disability as criteria that define the nature of one's relationship to the larger social community and the reciprocal duties that flow from it. While age or disability is sometimes relevant to one's ability to participate meaningfully in all aspects of the life of a community (e.g., voting, driving a car, viewing art exhibits), neither should ever be relevant to membership in the community in the first place. The touchstone for the legitimacy of using such factors depends on what one wants to use them for. This is the problem with Callahan's book.

The real question posed by Callahan in *Setting Limits* is this: "even though some treatments are technically feasible and will likely serve their intended purpose, should they nevertheless be denied to persons on the basis of age?" There is no easy answer to this question, but *Setting Limits* suggests two responses, both of which are equally evasive of the critical moral question of when the duty stops.

Neither a redefinition of the operative content of society's concept of the person nor the elaboration of an abstract concept of intergenerational equity provides an adequate response. Both seek to resolve a difficult moral dilemma by placing the focus on the individual for whom the treatment is sought. Neither addresses the issue of duty directly. If the duty can be avoided either because the patient is no longer to be considered a member of the community or because the elder can be accused of overstepping the bounds of intergenerational equity, then we will never reach the truly difficult question of how to balance our collective commitment to individual rights against our equally important (but far less considered) individual duty to refrain from making inequitable claims on the community. It is sad that the increasing cost of medical services has brought us to the brink of considering the elderly and the disabled as obstacles to social cohesiveness and progress, but, given our fixation on individual rights and our devotion to the cult of youth, it is not surprising. Old people simply get in the way.

Thus, the legal question that must be answered by Callahan is: for what purpose did you focus on the elderly and potential of those from whom you would withhold care? What is the end for which the suggested classification is to be used?[70]

Rethinking the Role of Autonomy

Is Autonomy the Basis of Community Membership?

We have now come full circle, to what might be considered the launchpad of Callahan's intended trajectory. What is the real reason for using age and age-related disability as a limit on health care? Although my full answer would require another paper, I here propose a brief answer.

Although *Setting Limits* may represent the first crack in the intellectual foundation of Callahan's view of individual rights, the capacity to act autonomously, that is, to reason, to have one's own emotions, and to form relationships, is the essence of one's humanity. Adopted as a key assumption of a public law, which rests on a natural rights view of the primacy and worth of the individual, the result is that the individualism condemned in *Setting Limits* replaces the more duty-based natural rights principles found in the Declaration of Independence and preamble to the Constitution of the United States as the foundation of public law. (This is especially true in what is known in constitutional law as the right to privacy.) Since autonomy is the ultimate personal right, dependency necessarily becomes the ultimate juridical and social tragedy. The social dying process has already begun, and for those with severe disabilities social death has already occurred. This is why one can treat a person in a persistent vegetative state as "[a] human bod[y] prior to clinical death."[71] Those who are no longer autonomous are simply "being[s],"[72] not people. This is why, in my judgment, it is fair to state that Callahan's actual subject is the rationing of health care on the basis of age and disability.

Although we approach the subject from very different starting points, Callahan and I thus agree that setting appropriate limits on personal autonomy is the great missing link in recent discussions of the rights of competent patients."[73] However, I would go one step further—and, implicitly, so does Callahan—to raise the ultimate question: do rights of autonomy and privacy even exist if their exercise is inconsistent with either justice or the common good? Thomas Jefferson gave us a hint when he said expressed his conviction that man "has no natural right in opposition to his social duties."[74]

Callahan is quite correct that even as the clamor continues for greater and greater freedom of choice in medical matters, the choices presented often amount to little more than a discussion of the merits or demerits of a given technological intervention. Moral concerns have given way to technological ones: "what can be done medically ought to be done."[75] Individual wants take precedence over human need.

That personal responsibility in matters of medical care has been ceded to a small army of medical professionals, lawyers, bureaucrats, cost-accountants, and sundry social engineers, including the U.S. Supreme Court,[76] cannot be denied. What is at issue is my contention that these surrogates have been invited (if not encouraged) to play the game strictly "by the numbers," and that Callahan's basic argument lends support to this trend. Only two questions are generally relevant to government officials in Washington and elsewhere: (1) who gets the money? (2) who is in charge? The political and practical truth is that whoever controls the money will be in charge.

A Suggested Approach: Social Duty and Personal Responsibility

Read together, the recent developments in the law of both aging and disability noted above stand for the proposition that the elderly and disabled are entitled, at a minimum, to equal treatment whenever they stand to receive the intended benefits of services offered to those without disabilities. Phrased another way, the burden is on those who would deny needed services to the elderly to do so on grounds demonstrably related to the individual case.

Thus, for equal protection purposes, there is no necessary connection between age per se and providing a lesser degree of legal protection or public services: age is both an over- and underinclusive classification. The same is true with respect to disability. Ultimately, the question is whether the most basic of public goods (protection from harm at the hands of others) will be apportioned on the basis of actual or presumed individual capacity. In my view, capacity cannot be the measure of membership in the community.

But none of this reaches the heart of Callahan's question "how much is enough?" I cannot answer that question, and I would argue strongly that society should not attempt to do so either. This question is, in fact, a question of duty, and the answer depends on the facts and circumstances of each case. "How much is enough?" is an impossible question to answer at the societal level.

What I can say is that before asking questions of broad social import, it is appropriate to focus on personal responsibility. The law is well equipped to scrutinize the legitimacy of the reasons given by individuals for their decisions. That they are personal (in the none-of-your-business sense) or medical (in the technical sense) makes little difference: patients, their families, medical professionals, bureaucrats, and legislators have arrogated to themselves a piece of a huge social program. Decisions that affect others must, at a minimum, be explained.

Conclusion

Callahan rightly questions the inevitable clash between claims for autonomy and the goal of setting limits on health care. Autonomy can be limited in only four basic ways: (1) exhortation (teaching) leading to self-control; (2) eliminating it altogether in certain instances (rationing); (3) limiting the class of persons who will be permitted to make valid claims (redefining personhood); or (4) moderating it with a competing operative principle of social relations (a social duty approach).

If rationing is necessary due to lack of resources and the legitimacy of competing demands, exhortation is out and a choice will be necessary from among the final two. But what choice? If individual autonomy is the highest value and there is no inclination to limit it as an operative principle of law and social relations (thus requiring otherwise autonomous individuals to justify some of their private choices), the logical (and most cost-effective) place to start is with those who are not autonomous. When the savings at that stage are exhausted, the next logical step is to consider potential (natural lifespan) and fairness (tolerable death) as criteria for rationing. Given the starting point and the desired target (rationing), the trajectory is obvious.

This is what is wrong with Callahan's trajectory. It scores a direct hit on those whom he claims to value, rather than upon the self-absorption he decries as the source of the problem. In my view, the advocates of Callahan's *Setting Limits* approach fail for the simple and wise observation made by the cartoon character Pogo: "We have met the Enemy and it is us!"[77] The wisdom of Jefferson's observation that there is no natural right in opposition to social duty has yet to be disproved, even if it remains unpopular at the moment. Striking a balance between autonomy and duty is always a delicate task, but *Setting Limits* is as good an argument as any about why we should get about the task as soon as possible. Excluding anyone, including the elderly, from the community simply will not do.

NOTES

1. Daniel Callahan, *Setting Limits: Medical Goals in an Aging Society* (New York: Simon and Schuster, 1987), 6.

2. Commenting on the repeal of the catastrophic health insurance program signed into law on July 1, 1988, Senator Alan K. Simpson of Wyoming noted that "the whole U.S. has been swung around on their tails by the 5.6 percent who don't want to pay for these benefits. . . . We[the Congress]'re not confused; we're terrorized. . . . Yeah, it's a social experiment; it's called pay for what you get." S. Rich, "Health Law Surtax Defeated; Senate Votes to Lower Catastrophic Benefits, But Rejects Repeal," Washington *Post,* Oct. 7, 1989, A1. The program was repealed in its entirety when Congress adjourned on Nov. 22, 1989. See T. Kenworthy and D. Phillips, "Hill to Face Health, Deficit Issues Anew; In Rush to Adjourn, Bills of Varying Significance Were Passed," Washington *Post,* Nov. 23, 1989, final ed., A4. See also, R. P. Hey, "Lawmakers Brace for Next Round on Health-Care Issue," *Christian Science Monitor,* Dec. 19, 1989, U.S. section, 7.

3. Callahan, *Setting Limits,* 52, 16–20, 37.

4. *County of Allegheny v. A.C.L.U.,* 492 U.S. 573, 109 S.Ct. 086, 3111 (1989). See *Webster v. Reproductive Health Services,* 492 U.S. 490, 109 S.Ct. 3040, 3079 (1989) (Stevens, J., concurring in part and dissenting in part). Cf. *Bowen v. Kendrick,* 484 U.S. 942 (1987).

5. Callahan, *Setting Limits,* 13, 141.

6. Ibid., 52.

7. See Ibid., 39. Callahan recognizes this problem in others when he notes that the starting point of the "seeds of the later ageism of the twentieth century were being sown" by those who "emphasi[zed] . . . the virtues of youth rather than age, the new rather than the old, self-reliance and autonomy rather than community. . . . But while repudiating ageism, we have not rejected those values which stimulated it in the first place."

8. See, e.g., ibid., 43: "Their indispensable role as conservators is what generates what I believe ought to be the *primary* aspiration of the old, which is to serve the young and the future" (emphasis in the original).

9. Cf. ibid., 47, quoting Edmund Burke's *Reflections on the Revolution in France* (London: Dent, 1910), 93–94: "Society is a partnership not only between those who are living, but those who are dead and those who are to be born."

10. Callahan, *Setting Limits,* 101 and n. 36, quoting M. Ignatieff, *The Needs of Strangers: An Essay on Privacy, Solidarity, and the Politics of Being Human* (New York: Viking Press, 1984), 52–53.

11. Compare the approach adopted by a majority of the U.S. Supreme Court in *Bowen v. American Hosp. Ass'n,* 476 U.S. 610 (1986) with that of the U.S. Commission on Civil Rights in *Medical Discrimination against Children with Disabilities* (Sept. 1989).

12. Callahan, *Setting Limits,* 10 (preface), 13 (ch. 1, "Health Care for the Elderly: How Much Is Enough?").

13. Included in this calculation is Callahan's view that medical care for the elderly takes place on the most technically advanced and costly frontier of medicine.

14. Ibid., 19.

15. Ibid., 183.

16. Ibid., 32–33.

17. Ibid., 32.

18. Ibid., 222, quoting Guido Calabresi and Philip Bobbitt, *Tragic Choices* (New York: W. W. Norton, 1978), 26.

19. Callahan, *Setting Limits,* 221.

20. Daniel Callahan, *What Kind of Life: The Limits of Medical Progress* (New York: Simon and Schuster, 1990), 12.

21. Ibid., 12, 30.

22. Ibid., 12.

23. Callahan, *Setting Limits,* 220.

24. Callahan correctly points out that "our secular morality (though perhaps not our religious traditions) provides few resources for living lives of unchosen obligations, those which through mischance lay upon us overwhelming [*sic*] demands to give our life over to the succor and welfare of someone else." Ibid., 96–97. What he ignores is that the "common coherent vision of the wellsprings of moral obligation toward the elderly in general and our elderly parents in particular" we "lack" must either be developed afresh or redeveloped from nonsecular sources.

25. *Strauder v. West Virginia,* 100 U.S. 303, 307–8 (1880).

26. U.S. Const. Amend. XIV 1 (1868).

27. See, e.g., *Plyler v. Doe,* 457 U.S. 202 (1982); *San Antonio School Ind. Dist. v. Rodriguez,* 411 U.S. 1 (1973).

28. See, e.g., *Metro Broadcasting Co. v. F.C.C.,* __ U.S. __, 110 S.Ct. 2997 (1990); *Astroline Communications v. Shurberg Broadcasting,* __ U.S. __, 110 S.Ct. 1316 (1990); *Martin v. Wilks,* 490 U.S. 755 (1989) (5-4 decision); *Lorance v. A.T. & T. Technologies, Inc.,* 490 U.S. 900 (1989) (6-3 decision); *Patterson v. McLean Credit Union,* 491 U.S. 164 (1989) (6-3 on the disputed issues); *Wards Cove Packing Co., Inc. v. Atonio,* 490 U.S. 642 (1989) (5-4 decision); *City of Richmond v. J. A. Croson Co., Inc.,* 488 U.S. 469 (1989) (5-4 decision). Compare S. 2104 and H.R. 4000, 101st Cong. 2d Sess. (The Civil Rights Act of 1990) and 136 Cong. Rec. S.991-01 (Feb. 7, 1990) (remarks of Senator Kennedy) with 136 Cong. Rec. S.457-07 (Jan. 29, 1990) (remarks of Senator Hatch). See also H.R. 3035, 3455, 101st Cong., 1st Sess. (1989) (proposed amendments to the civil rights laws in light of the foregoing cases).

29. This explains in part the U.S. Supreme Court's unwillingness to require the government to provide the means by which such rights can be enjoyed. See, e.g., *Harris v. McRae,* 448 U.S. 297 (1980).

30. Some of the most intractable problems in American constitutional law have been caused, in part, by the U.S. Supreme Court's unwillingness to read the equal protection clause as a standard of conduct for those not claiming its protection. See, e.g., *Brown v. Board of Education* (II), 349 U.S. 294 (1955) (remedial phase: "all deliberate speed"); *Korematsu v. United States,* 323 U.S. 214 (1944) (Japanese internment); *Plessy v. Ferguson,* 163 U.S. 537 (1896) ("separate but equal").

31. A similar duty has been imposed by statute upon certain individuals and institutions for the benefit of persons who are deemed to be particularly at risk. See, e.g., Title VII of the *Civil Rights Act of 1964,* 42 U.S.C. § 2000e, et. seq.; *Age Discrimination in Employment Act* (ADEA), 29 U.S.C. §§ 621–633a (1989).

32. See, e.g., *Texas Monthly v. Bullock,* 489 U.S. 1 (1989); *Lyng v. Northwest Indian Cemetery Protective Assn,* 481 U.S. 1036 (1987); *Regan v. Taxation with Representation of Washington,* 461 U.S. 540, 544, 549 (1983); *Abood v. Detroit Board of Education,* 431 U.S. 209 (1977).

33. See, e.g., *City of Richmond v. J. A. Croson Co., Inc.,* 109 S.Ct. 706 (1989) (nonremedial affirmative action); *San Antonio School Ind. Dist. v. Rodriguez,* 411 U.S. 1 (1973) (equalization of public school resource allocations).

34. See *Plyler v. Doe,* 457 U.S. 202 (1982).

35. See *City of Cleburne, Texas v. Cleburne Living Center, Inc.,* 473 U.S. 432 (1985) (invalidating a statute on the basis of "an irrational prejudice against the mentally retarded").

36. This also accounts for the deep divisions in society over quota-based affirmative action plans in civil rights. The dispute is over the nature of government obligations to those whom the law considers deserving of special protection against discrimination (i.e., minorities), and those who are to be treated under generally applicable standards governing social conduct. Detailed examination of this topic, however, is beyond the scope of this paper.

37. E.g., Callahan, *Setting Limits,* 115: "What is the extent of the government's obligation. Or, to put the matter more precisely, what is the extent of our common

obligation as a society using the instruments of government to provide health care for the elderly?"

38. There is, in fact, a third and critically important question: "whose duty is it?" Although Callahan discusses it extensively, a critique of his answer is beyond the scope of this paper.

39. See, e.g., R. Destro, foreword, " 'The Religious Foundations of Civil Rights Law' and the Study of Law and Religion in an Interdisciplinary Framework" in a symposium entitled The Religious Foundations of Civil Rights Law, *Journal of Law and Religion* 5 (1987): 39; R. Destro, "Equality, Social Welfare and Equal Protection," *Harvard Journal of Law and Public Policy* 9 (1986):53.

40. See, e.g., *Roe v. Wade,* 410 U.S. 113 (1973). See also R. Destro, "Abortion and the Constitution: The Need for a Life-Protective Amendment," *California Law Review* 63 (1975): 1250, 1282–92 (discussing the history of the Fourteenth Amendment's concept of "person"); J. A. Parness, "Social Commentary: Values and Legal Personhood," *West Virginia Law Review* 83 (1982):487 (arguing that the interests of others would be adversely affected by conferring legal personhood on the unborn). See generally R. B. Stewart, "Federalism: Allocating Responsibility Between the Federal and State Courts," *Georgia Law Review* 19 (1985): 917, 932, and n. 45 (differentiating between status as a "citizen" and as a "person" with respect to basic rights); D. R. Ratner, "Corporations and the Constitution," *University of San Francisco Law Review* 15 (1981):11; Note, "Constitutional Rights of the Corporate Person," *Yale Law Journal* 81 (1982): 1641.

41. Callahan, *Setting Limits,* 179.

42. Ibid., 179–80.

43. 98 N.J. 321, 486 A.2d. 1209 (1985).

44. 108 N.J. 394, 529 A.2d 434 (1987).

45. 110 S.Ct. 2841 (1990).

46. Callahan, *Setting Limits,* 182.

47. The implications of Callahan's views for the status of unborn children are beyond the scope of this paper.

48. The natural rights argument is developed at greater length in two articles: R. Destro, "Guaranteeing a Minimum Quality of Life through Law: The Emerging Right to a Good Life," *This World* 25 (Spring 1989): 73, and R. Destro, "Quality of Life Ethics and Constitutional Jurisprudence: The Demise of Natural Rights and Equal Protection for the Disabled and Incompetent," *Journal of Contemporary Health Law and Policy* 2 (1986): 71.

49. Callahan, *Setting Limits,* 184.

50. Ibid.

51. Ibid., 220. There are, however, exceptions to every rule. In certain circumstances, such behavior is, in fact, gradually becoming more tolerable, but only because the reality of the acts or omissions is masked behind arguments for personal autonomy. See, e.g., *Cruzan v. Harmon,* 760 S.W.2d 408 (1988) (en banc) cert. granted 109 S.Ct. 3240 (1989); *Bowen v. American Hosp. Ass'n,* 476 U.S. 610 (1986); *State by Bowers v. McAffee,* 259 Ga. 579; 385 S.E.2d 651 (1989). This is evidence not of a lack of moral and cultural resources, but of a shift in the tenor of the debate. Such evasion is not a welcome development for

those who have devoted years to altering societal attitudes toward persons with disabilities.

52. Callahan, *Setting Limits,* 183.

53. Callahan and others have argued that an unborn child might become a subject of legal protection as its brain develops, that is, as its potential increases. See Daniel Callahan, *Abortion: Law, Choice and Morality* (New York: Doubleday, 1970), 378–409, and B. Brody, *Abortion and the Sanctity of Human Life: A Philosophical View* (Cambridge, Mass.: MIT Press, 1975), 100–115. For a critical view of Callahan's moral argument see, e.g., P. Ramsey, "Abortion: A Review Article," *The Thomist* 37 (Jan. 1973): 174–226.

54. R. Neuhaus, "Nihilism without the Abyss: Law, Rights, and Transcendent Good," in a symposium entitled The Religious Foundations of Civil Rights Law, *Journal of Law and Religion* 5 (1987): 53, 57 [referring to *Roe v. Wade,* 410 U.S. 113 (1973)].

55. Callahan, *Setting Limits,* 66.

56. Section 504 of the Rehabilitation Act of 1973, 29 U.S.C. Section 794 (1989).

57. P.L. 101-336, 104 Stat. 327, codified at 42 U.S.C. §§ 12101–12213 (1990). The act was signed by President Bush on July 27, 1990.

58. Americans with Disabilities Act, Section 301 (7)(F), 42 U.S.C. § 12181 (7)(F) (1990).

59. Beginning with the Older Americans Act in 1965, 42 U.S.C. § 3001 (1989), and continuing with the enactment of the Age Discrimination in Employment Act (ADEA), 29 U.S.C. §§ 621–633a (1989), the U.S. Congress has expressed a clear policy that the elderly should be accorded both the attention required by their special needs and equality of treatment in the work place. A number of recent cases expand the coverage of the ADEA. See, e.g., *Gregory v. Ashcroft,* 898 F.2d 598 (8th Cir. 1990) (application of ADEA to mandatory retirement of state judges); *E.E.O.C. v. State of New York,* 729 F. Supp. 266 (S.D. N.Y. 1990) (same); *E.E.O.C. v. State of Illinois,* 721 F. Supp. 156 (N.D. Ill, 1989) (same); *E.E.O.C. v. State of Vermont,* 717 F. Supp. 26 (D. Vt. 1989) (same); *Myrick v. Devils Lake Sioux Mfg. Corp.,* 718 F. Supp. 753 (D.N.D. 1989) (application of ADEA to Indian tribal entities); *E.E.O.C. v. Cherokee Nation,* 1989 WL 83776 (E.D. Okl.), 49 *Fair Empl.Prac.Cas.* (BNA) 1072 (E.D.Okl., 1988) (same).

60. See: *Alexander v. Choate,* 469 U.S. 287, 105 S.Ct. 712, 718–20 (1985) (holding that Section 504 would clearly cover cases of intentional discrimination against the handicapped, but refusing to hold either that the regulations promulgated under the statute are limited to such cases or that the statute necessarily comprehends the use of "disparate impact" analysis); *Consolidated Rail Corp. v. Darrone,* 465 U.S. 624 (1984) (coverage of funded programs); *Smith v. Robinson,* 468 U.S. 992 (1984).

61. *Alexander v. Choate,* 469 U.S. 287, 296, 105 S.Ct. 712, 718, and nn. 12–16. (1985). The sources cited by the court make it clear that it was drawing a bright line between "thoughtlessness and indifference" that, though neglecting the needs of the disabled, might be considered "benign" in that they are not intentional, and that which is truly "invidious."

62. U.S. Commission on Civil Rights, *Medical Discrimination against Children with Disabilities,* supra note 11, ch. 1–3, 9–10.

63. Compare, e.g., *Bowen v. American Hosp. Ass'n,* 476 U.S. 610 (1986); *In re Estate of Longeway v. Community Convalescent Center,* 133 Ill. 2d 33, 549 N.E.2d 292 (1989); and *State by Bowers v. McAffee,* 259 Ga. 579; 385 S.E.2d 651 (1989), *In re Conroy,* 98 N.J. 321, 486 A.2d. 1209 (1985) with *In re O'Connor,* 72 N.Y.2d 517, 531 N.E.2d 607, 534 N.Y.S.2d 886 (1988), *In the Matter of Doris Wickel v. Spellman,* No. 2359E, 1990 N.Y. App. Div. LEXIS 2746, (Sup. Ct. App. Div., 2d Dept., filed March 12, 1990); *Cruzan v. Harmon,* 760 S.W.2d 408 (1988) (en banc) cert. granted 109 S.Ct. 3240 (1989).

64. Callahan, *Setting Limits,* 168.

65. See, generally, *A.B.A. Model Code of Professional Responsibility* (Chicago: American Bar Association, 1989).

66. See Callahan, *Setting Limits,* ch. 6, "Allocating Resources to the Elderly," and ch. 7, "Care of the Elderly Dying."

67. Ibid., 168.

68. See note *supra,* quoting ibid., 222.

69. The state of Oregon has recently adopted a plan for explicit rationing of health care. See W. King, "Cancer Treatment: Who Gets Left Out?" Seattle *Times,* Jan. 31, 1990, B1; R.S. Boyd, "Rationing Health Care," ibid., Jan. 8, 1990, F1. See also Editorial, "Rational Maybe, Moral Never: Health Care Shortages Vividly Illustrate Heartbreaking Dilemma," Los Angeles *Times,* May 5, 1990, B6, col. 3 (discussing failed attempt by Alameda County/Oakland, Calif., to set up a health-care rationing program).

70. In equal protection parlance, this is known as the "means-end fit." The U.S. Supreme Court has resisted making what is, in effect, a moral rule under the equal protection clause that age and disability are inherently illegitimate (i.e., constitutionally suspect) classifications because there are times when they are demonstrably legitimate criteria for private and public decision-making. See, e.g., *City of Cleburne, Texas v. Cleburne Living Center, Inc.,* 473 U.S. 432 (1985) (invalidating a statute on the basis of "an irrational prejudice against the mentally retarded").

71. Callahan, *Setting Limits,* 182.

72. Ibid.

73. Ibid., 176.

74. From the letter to the Danbury Baptist Association, *Works of Thomas Jefferson,* ed. H. Washington (1861), 8:113.

75. Callahan, *Setting Limits,* 17.

76. *Bowen v. American Hosp. Ass'n,* 476 U.S. 610 (1986); *Roe v. Wade,* 410 U.S. 113 (1973). See *Cruzan v. Director, Missouri Department of Health,* __ U.S. __, 110 S.Ct. 2841 (1990), aff'd; *Cruzan v. Harmon,* 760 S.W.2d 408 (1988) (en banc).

77. The Pogo cartoon series was drawn and written by the late Walt Kelly.

PART THREE

---

*Public Policy and Economic
Aspects of Age-Based
Rationing*

5

Rationing Health Care:
Legal Issues and Alternatives
to Age-Based Rationing

MARSHALL KAPP

Wishing and hoping will not solve the problem of an American health-care system whose costs are out of control.[1] Eventually public demand and need (concepts that are not logically distinct but are politically almost synonymous) for medical services will exceed our society's economic capacity (not just our willingness) to satisfy that appetite. Try as we might to avoid it, the "R" word[2]—rationing—must eventually be confronted in all its ethical, legal, and political dimensions.

Even if rationing cannot be avoided altogether, however, the scarcity of medical resources relative to demand that might prompt rationing can at least be mitigated. To the extent that use of available medical resources is optimized, the point at which the most gripping rationing dilemmas must be confronted would be altered, and the severity of rationing strategies possibly softened. The need for rationing would remain, but the nature of its legal, ethical, and political implications would be altered. Thus, while working on the supply side of the equation will not by itself resolve the rationing issue in a completely satisfactory way, it can exert a fundamental impact on how society chooses to deal with the demand side.

What alternatives, then, are feasible for delaying and/or mitigating the scarcity of resources and hence the necessity of rationing? First, we could spend more on health care, both in absolute dollars and as a percentage of gross national product. Although eventually we would find ourselves broke yet desirous of more health care, pouring more money into the coffers would push back the threshold at which the most troubling rationing dilemmas become unavoidable. This alternative is neither politically feasible for the foreseeable future nor, probably, socially desirable, for we would merely postpone the debate on the ethical, legal, and political ramifications of resource scarcity for education, welfare, national defense, the physical infrastructure, and so on.

One method of optimizing the use of scarce medical resources, which is both politically feasible and legally and economically desirable, is the elimination of futile, nonbeneficial medical interventions. There is no obligation on any ground to provide futile treatments to patients.[3] Before we progress—or regress, depending on one's perspective—to rationing schemes based on cost/benefit analyses, involving ethically loaded judgments about comparative need and social equity, we ought first to look toward ferreting out medical interventions that carry with them no likelihood of benefit at all.[4]

In this sphere there is the growing attention among governmental and foundation sponsors of health services research, as well as in various medical professional organizations, to the process of better technology assessment and the development of better clinical standards founded on empirical evidence about which interventions contribute to positive patient outcomes.[5] This technology assessment/clinical standard-setting trend—recognition of the physician's obligation as specialist[6]—holds the promise of eliminating many costly medical practices whose usages are due more to habit, history, irrational fear of litigation, and reimbursement incentives than to any convincing proof of medical efficacy. Significant medical resources (even if never totally enough) could thus be transferred to those patients in which intervention promised a greater chance of success. A salutary by-product of the process of clinical standard-setting would be improvement in the malpractice climate for providers.[7]

Another method of reducing the provision of futile, nonbeneficial medical interventions and thus enhancing the availability of resources for positive purposes is to encourage a more complete disclosure to patients, families, and even medical professionals about the likely inefficacy in many situations of expensive, as well intrusive, medical interventions. Examples include cardiopulmonary resuscitation (CPR) and intensive care units (ICUs). At risk here is a popular, and often erroneous, perception that the higher the technology—and the more of it—the higher the quality of medical care. In fact, if patients, their families,[8] and their physicians were privy to more complete information about the proven inefficacy of certain advanced medical technologies in particular circumstances, as well as the very frequent negative prognoses associated with the use of such technologies, such medical interventions would be declined more often and appreciable resources could be conserved.[9] Advance directives such as living wills and durable powers of attorney for health care could be utilized to document patient wishes to limit future medical intervention.[10] Referring specifically to older persons—the chief focus of this chapter—one British observer of the American health scene has noted, "The inappropriate deployment of medical interventions, insofar as it occurs, is not impelled by the demands of the elderly or their families so much as by professionals setting the wrong objectives or working under extraneous and unnecessary pressures from the administrative arrangements for funding or the fear of litigation."[11]

A related strategy would be to encourage, indeed to enforce, more respect by physicians and health-care facility administrators for the wishes of patients and families to limit aggressive, expensive medical interventions at the end of life where, in the value calculus of the patient and family, the foreseeable burdens of continued treatment outweigh the benefits.[12] I have suggested recently that, to both foster patient autonomy and to save money for more beneficial medical purposes, third-party reimbursement for medical services ought to be linked to demonstration of informed consent to those services, so that interventions for which there exists no clear documentation of informed consent by an authorized decision-maker would be uncompensated.[13] A recent New York decision disallowing a nursing home's bill for unconsented-to ventilator care of a patient seems to support the reasoning of this proposal.[14]

Professor Robert Schwartz has suggested:

> If we respect the autonomy of those terrorized [by the fear of being kept alive but debilitated indefinitely by medical technology] patients and their long suffering families and refrain from providing them the treatment they do not want, we will go a long way towards overcoming the problem. Before we impose terror on the elderly who do not want to die, we ought to respect their wishes and avoid the terror of those who believe that their time to die has come. In fact, limiting health care choices, if necessary at all, can be tailored to the needs of individual patients. . . . much of the end sought by [proponents of rationing according to age] can be achieved through the *recognition* of autonomy, not by its *limitation*. If those who wish to forego treatment—those now "terrorized" by the prospect of its imposition—are permitted to have their wishes honored, a great deal of the medical treatment [age-based rationing proponents] find unwarranted by its expense will cease.[15]

In the final analysis, however, even if the strategies proposed for mitigating the resource scarcity problem succeed, their implementation would only delay, not eliminate, the rationing conundrum.[16] These strategies would be valuable, but not sufficient. There is still only so much wasteful and inappropriate treatment to be squeezed out of the system,[17] especially where older patients, who understandably consume a disproportionate amount of health-care resources,[18] are involved. Even Daniel Callahan has admitted that "right now, the very old do not receive a great deal of high-technology medicine"[19] for the treatment of acute problems; instead, most expenditures for the elderly are devoted to long-term care of chronic disabilities and ailments (although there is a trend toward consumption of more high-technology care by the elderly, in addition to—not in place of—maintenance care for chronic conditions).[20] Reluctantly but inevitably, we must turn our attention to an exploration of different rationing methods and their political, legal, and ethical dimensions.

Methods of Explicit Rationing

There are essentially three ways in which rationing of medical services as a means of controlling expenditures might be achieved. Most drastically, government could outlaw the provision of specified medical services (e.g., heart transplants) to specified groups of patients (e.g., people over sixty-five years old), at any price and regardless of source of payment. Neither the patient, the physician, nor any other gatekeeper would possess discretion in this model. Some philosophical proposals for age-based rationing according to age, such as Robert Veatch's "egalitarian justice over a lifetime" theory, which posits a straight priority claim to medical resources in inverse proportion to chronological age[21] (the "Fair Innings" concept), and Norman Daniels's "Prudential Lifespan Account" for rationing by age group but not by cohort,[22] could be interpreted as supporting this approach. However, a governmental prohibition on the private sale or purchase of specified medical services would almost undoubtedly run afoul of both the provider's and potential patient's substantive due process rights to be treated in a nonarbitrary and noncapricious manner.[23]

Two other approaches would not ban specified treatments outright, but would deny or limit financial payment for specified services according to the age, disease, or other distinguishing characteristics of the patient. The burden of choice would be shifted to the patient, family, and physician. Since the patient will seldom have sufficient resources to pay for desired services out-of-pocket, this choice may be more hypothetical than real, with a result of rationing by economics.

The two reimbursement-related rationing approaches differ according to the type of third-party payor involved. In one approach, private insurance corporations determine the coverage the beneficiaries of their insurance policies receive. This process is already in operation, although decisions today are based upon treatment modalities (e.g., psychotherapy versus inpatient psychiatric hospitalization) and provider identity (e.g., obstetrician versus midwife) rather than patient characteristics. This approach highlights the fact that much of what we think of as public health policy in actuality is made by private actors. This dynamic, characteristic of much of American life, has as its chief detriment the removal of important rationing decisions from effective public scrutiny and political accountability. While we have the right to vote for or against elected officials, as citizens we have no say about who will make benefits decisions on behalf of private insurance companies and employers that will affect health-care availability for millions of individuals.

In the second approach, public health-care financing programs exclude provider reimbursement for certain kinds of intervention for some specified otherwise covered population groups.[24] In the context of Callahan's much-discussed call for reimbursement-related rationing of medical services strictly according to the patient's chronological age,[25] this approach takes the form of restrictions on Medicare[26] (and to a lesser extent Medicaid[27]) coverage for specified treatments. Public entitlements to medical services would thus be limited.[28]

These rationing methodologies raise questions of a political, legal, and ethical nature. Because it is the proposal that has attracted the most attention thus far and probably stands the greatest possibility of general acceptance, Callahan's public reimbursement rationing scheme based upon chronological age serves as the focus of the following analysis.[29]

Before moving to that analysis, though, I should note that I do not attempt to deal directly with private rationing decisions made by individual physicians regarding individual patients at the bedside. Although there is a widespread understanding that this practice occurs everyday in our health-care system, based on individual physician calculations of relative costs and benefits, there is a general reluctance to publicly acknowledge this private rationing for fear that such actions may expose individual physicians to potential legal liability for malpractice.[30] That legal apprehension may be well founded[31] or not.[32] It also has been suggested that private rationing decisions by a physician or institution based on the patient's age might constitute a violation of the federal Age Discrimination Act (ADA).[33] The merits of these legal issues and of the ethical justifications or condemnations of this practice of bedside rationing[34] are beyond the scope of this chapter. Rather, I focus here only on formal, explicit rationing programs enacted and implemented by the government.

Political and Legal Dimensions

Political Dimensions

The call by Callahan and others[35] for an explicit public policy of age-based health-care rationing did not spawn, but ideologically feeds and fits nicely within, the intergenerational equity movement (led by Americans for Generational Equity, or AGE), which is generating increasing attention in public policy-making corridors.[36] The political rallying cry of this private lobbying movement is that a public dollar spent on the elderly (for health care or any other reason) is a dollar diverted away from services devoted to other age groups, especially the young.[37] According to this logic, we cannot begin to fulfill our societal responsibilities to properly educate, feed, house, and medically care for the next generation—a disproportionately high number of whom are growing up in severe poverty—without diminishing public benefits (both income maintenance like Social Security retirement payments[38] and in-kind payments like Medicare and Medicaid) now being lavished upon the elderly regardless of personal need. Callahan refers to this as the "blocking" principle—that is, entitlements for the elderly "block" opportunities for other groups.[39]

To the extent they are able to propel this argument (which, incidentally, is predicated on several debatable factual premises concerning the financial well-being of older citizens)[40] into the public arena, generational equity proponents engender a controversy that, within our pluralistic political system of rough and tumble private interest groups vigorously competing with each other, will jeopardize the implicit social equilibrium that holds us together.[41] It is ironic that Callahan and his supporters attempt to buttress their proposal on the argument that forcing involuntary medical sacrifices on the elderly to benefit youth will somehow foster a stronger ideal of general community. In reality, political warring over age-based rationing is far more likely to encourage bitterly divisive selfishness by particular age cohorts, even among individuals within the same cohort (as the recent debacle involving repeal of the Medicare Catastrophic Care Act[42] nicely illustrates), in quest of preserving one's own piece of the medical pie than would continued recognition of the mutual interdependence of generations.[43]

Legal Dimensions

The political and ethical ramifications of the age-based health-care rationing concept have received a fair amount of commentary.[44] Conversely, extensive discussion of the legal issues raised by a public policy of discrimination against the elderly in access to medical services (as opposed to literature speculating about the potential liability of physicians and hospitals that de facto scrimp on care to particular older individuals under present cost-containment pressures like prospective payment according to diagnosis-related groups)[45] has been late in coming.

This analytical void is at least partially explained by the paucity of specific detail that the philosophical promoters of age-based rationing provide to describe how their general policies of formal medical discrimination would be implemented in practice. Since good legal analysis always begins with a mastery of the facts, the factual abyss that characterizes the arguments of Callahan et al.—the failure to move very far from theory into practice—deters speculation about the legal implications of those arguments. Nonetheless, it appears inevitable that the courts will become involved in the health-care rationing policy debate. According to Robert Blank, "Unless one defines policymaking very narrowly, the courts always have and will continue to make policy through their decisions." Since, in his estimate, the courts are the "primary guarantors of individual rights" against government intrusion, health-care rationing is an obvious and inescapable arena for judicial activism.[46] Thus, a few brief surmises about probable legal challenges to a public policy embodying categorical,[47] age-based health-care rationing are offered here.

First, the Fifth and Fourteenth Amendments to the U.S. Constitution guarantee that no individual may be deprived by the government of life, liberty, or property without due process of law. In both substantive and procedural terms, this means that persons are entitled to be treated in a fundamentally fair way by their government. A governmental scheme to utilize reimbursement policy to deprive, consciously and officially, older persons, solely because of their age, of access to potentially beneficial health services raises two sorts of due process questions (assuming that a property right indeed is implicated, that is, that government has some duty to provide access to health-care services).[48]

First, aging is an immutable,[49] involuntary, uncontrollable contingency of life. As James Childress has noted, "Ageism, like racism and sexism, involves a set of beliefs, attitudes, and practices that unjustly and unjustifiably discriminate against a group. We have no responsibility for our aging; if we live long enough, we will age. On at least one level, then, ageism is comparable to racism and sexism and should be rejected for similar reasons, which also appear to exclude the use of age as a criterion for the distribution of medical care."[50] Predicating a public-benefits rationing scheme upon chronological age, therefore, is arguably an arbitrary and capricious exercise of governmental authority, involving denial of a property[51] right that is not adequately supported by a reasonable relationship between that denial and a legitimate government interest.[52]

A second concern could be based on the phenomenon that many older persons are institutionalized, under explicit or implicit government sanction, in mental hospitals or long-term care facilities that are either owned and operated by the government or are heavily supported by public funds; many older persons have had decision-making powers removed via guardianship or conservator appointments by the courts; and other kinds of limitations on the liberty of older persons may be imposed by government. Should not the elderly be entitled, as a due process quid pro quo for these deprivations of freedom by the government, to something in return, namely, to be provided with the basics of life, including potentially beneficial medical care?[53] A closely analogous treatment-as-quid-pro-quo-for-deprivation-of-freedom argument has been accepted by the courts as a

constitutional principle in the contexts of involuntary mental hospitalization[54] and imprisonment.[55]

If age-based rationing of Medicare benefits were implemented through an
administrative agency like the federal Health Care Financing Administration,
procedural due process protections would be implicated. Procedural due
process guarantees beneficiaries whose government benefit is adversely
affected by an action of an administrative agency a right to notification of
the agency action and to a hearing to challenge that action.[56] That challenge will turn on a balancing of beneficiary and governmental interests
and also consideration of the extent to which procedural protections will
safeguard the beneficiary's interest. Given the fairly narrow view of procedural due process protections for Medicare beneficiaries taken thus far by
the courts,[57] a challenge to age-based rationing predicated on this argument may not succeed.[58]

An official age-based health-care rationing program might also be
attacked by the elderly as a deprivation of the equal protection rights
guaranteed to all persons by the Fifth[59] and Fourteenth Amendments.[60]
Without doubt, the kind of policy advocated by Callahan involves intentional discrimination by the government against a particular category of
people, based exclusively on their membership in that category.[61] The
critical constitutional inquiry is can an age-based health-care rationing
policy be justified as an exception to the general equal protection mandate.

Equal protection analysis asks whether the government can demonstrate
a rational relationship between its differential treatment of different groups
and a legitimate public interest. Even under this test, it is debatable
whether the government's choice of age as the distinguishing characteristic
for rationing health care would pass constitutional scrutiny.

Moreover, an official age-based health-care rationing scheme ought to
be subjected to a higher level of equal protection analysis, that of "strict
scrutiny."[62] Under this test, the government bears the burden of proving
that its policy of discriminating among citizen groups is necessary (not just
rationally related) to accomplish a compelling (not just a legitimate) public
interest. The courts have engaged in strict scrutiny analysis when either a
fundamental (not just an important) right is the subject of deprivation or
the group being discriminated against is a "suspect class."

Although the courts thus far have resisted categorizing it as such,[63]
beneficial health care ought to be considered a fundamental right, at least
as encompassed in the Medicare program. The core value of the Medicare
program's ideology is that health care is special in a way that other goods
and services are not.[64]

Additionally, although the courts have not yet recognized old age as a
"suspect class" for equal protection purposes,[65] they should,[66] just as the

use of another immutable, involuntary category—race—has been presumed constitutionally improper.[67] Age-based rationing proposals are an excellent example of the vulnerability of the elderly qua elderly to the adverse effects of discriminatory public policy decisions. It is unlikely that a comprehensive, inflexible age-based health-care rationing program of the sort envisioned by Callahan could withstand a strict scrutiny analysis.

Even if an official policy of rationing health care by age survived these analyses, it would still need to satisfy the equal protection principle that it be the least invasive, least restrictive alternative reasonably available and that it is likely to be effective in achieving a justifiable aim.[68] Thus, proponents of an age-based health-care rationing scheme shoulder the difficult if not impossible burden of establishing both that their scheme was adopted only as a last resort after other, less invasive and restrictive cost containment measures (such as those suggested earlier in this article) were properly rejected as ineffectual, and that an age-based rationing program is likely to be effective in achieving the goals of effective cost containment and otherwise improving quality and access within the health-care system. Callahan attempts to justify his proposal on precisely this ground—that in return for involuntarily foregoing life-sustaining, technologically oriented medical interventions the elderly will have access to a more appropriate mix of services, including good long-term care.[69] James Blumstein's analysis of Callahan's proposal, however, implies a constitutional vulnerability in the absence of a showing of valuable benefit to the elderly as a quid pro quo for their deprivations.[70] Blumstein also warns that while age-based rationing of health care might withstand equal protection scrutiny on its face, a different result might ensue from unfairness in the application of limits to particular persons in specific circumstances.[71]

Other constitutional challenges to age-based health-care rationing might surface to be voiced also. The constitutional prohibition against governmental interference with freedom of contract[72] that has been read into the Fourteenth Amendment's liberty protection clause might be asserted against any law purporting to outlaw the provision of certain services to the elderly as an impermissible interference with the physician/patient relationship.[73] A similar attack might be mounted against a Callahan-type proposal (rationing based on payment restrictions) since, even where (as in Medicare) the government is paying the bills, the contractual (as well as the fiduciary) relationship is one that exists between the patient and the private health-care provider.

The same reasoning may support a challenge to age-based health-care rationing under the constitutional right of privacy that has been recognized as incorporating the freedom to make personal health-care decisions without governmental interference.[74] While establishing an affirmative entitlement to government-funded health-care benefits might be difficult to accomplish under the right to privacy rubric,[75] at the least the privacy claim should protect the right of an older individual to pay for desired services if willing and able.

Ethical Dimensions

Ethical Justifications

It should be admitted that there is a strong argument in favor of the idea of rationing health care according to age. As critics of our present health-care system insist, the United States already rations some medical services to a large extent in an implicit, or "soft," fashion.[76] (Nations with socialized medicine systems, such as Great Britain, use such implicit rationing methods as categorizing certain kinds of care for certain kinds of patients as "not medically indicated" as a fundamental tool of cost containment.[77]) This usually occurs on an unspoken financial basis (e.g., if a person cannot afford, through personal assets or insurance, to pay for a service, he or she may not receive that service, at least in the manner and from the provider of choice).[78]

Implicit rationing is not always economically determined. For example, we ration care according to geographical factors or a patient's particular disease.[79] Further, empirical studies show that many physicians now use age per se as a treatment criterion, that is, age as a proxy for medical and social factors in making triage determinations about the intergenerational allocation of scarce resources.[80] The argument goes that if we accept the inevitability of health rationing according to some process and some criteria,[81] it is ethically preferable to establish the process and criteria explicitly, through public discourse and in ways subject to public accountability ("hard" rationing).[82]

Callahan and others may be correct that explicit or hard rationing is preferable to implicit or soft rationing because the former subjects decisions and actions and the rationales and premises underlying them to public scrutiny and debate.[83] Society must finally grapple with the issue of scarce medical resources being overwhelmed by need, let alone desire. However, for the political and legal reasons noted above and the ethical objections to follow, an explicit official program of health-care rationing based on age is not the answer.

Ethical Objections

One serious criticism of the Callahan proposal is that an official policy of discrimination against the aged scapegoats and symbolically devalues them both in their own eyes and in the eyes of others.[84] Rationing is much more than simply a mechanism of cost containment.[85] A nation's health policy reflects and influences broader social values and attitudes toward vulnerable groups.[86] A policy of hard rationing according to chronological years would reflect a lack of respect for the aged.[87] Allocating fewer resources for medical care for the aged might imply a reduction in the applicable standard of care pertaining to patients in that age group.[88] Callahan has accused the older cohort of setting a poor example of stewardship for the young, by too voraciously consuming health-care resources that ought better be left for succeeding generations.[89] Should we not ask, though, whether there is not a duty of stewardship to pass along to our youth a spirit of respect for the value and humanity of their elders, a spirit that age-based rationing can only weaken?

If we devalue the elderly in this context, a ripple effect would establish a mindset that would make it easier to deny other kinds of services to the elderly or to other dependent groups. General life expectations would be diminished, both for those who are already old and for those contemplating their old age. Professionals, institutions, and agencies that care for the elderly would be diminished in stature as well as budget, with a definite diminution in the enthusiasm and performance quality they bring to their "dumping ground" role.[90] This is the beginning of a slippery slope that would be difficult to ungrease. One scholar has advocated abolishing a government program altogether rather than permitting its conditions to devalue one particular segment of the population.[91]

Another ethical difficulty with age-based rationing is the serious damage to the physician/patient relationship that would be wrought by thrusting physicians into the double agent role of societal gatekeeper versus zealous advocate for the individual patient.[92] Some physicians support a strict global rationing scheme, on the theory that depriving both physicians and patients of utilization choices removes physicians from the "moral hook" that the power to make difficult decisions creates. Patients are not likely to see matters that way; instead, they will—or could—grow to distrust physicians whether the latter are the architects of society's rationing scheme or only the instruments who carry it out.

Third, for the past quarter century society has created, through Medicare and Medicaid, a legitimate expectation on the part of both older and younger people that to a large extent it will financially assist older persons to secure access to high-quality health care. Important decisions about savings and consumption by both old and young individuals are made according to the expectations so fostered. Would it be just, even on the prospective basis proposed by Callahan (the prospectivity greatly diminishing the value of the purported savings), to renege on that expectation? Does an intentionally created, reasonable expectation of societal help create a legitimate dependency that, in turn, should translate into an individual entitlement that, in turn, equals a public obligation or commitment?

Fourth, as noted in the earlier discussion about due process, society limits the personal freedoms of many older persons in a variety of ways. These intrusions into individual liberty often are more de facto than de jure as, for instance, where a family admits its older relative to a nursing home on a superficially voluntary basis. Frequently these limitations of freedom are necessary and proper to promote the principle of beneficence. However, on an ethical as well as a due process basis, are not older persons whose freedom has been formally or informally compromised entitled to claim adequate medical services from society in return? Does the principle of justice support paternalism when it comes to limiting the autonomy of the elderly, but rugged individualism when it comes to their medical care?

Finally (although this list is by no means intended as comprehensive), age-based health-care rationing should be faulted for its erroneous assumption of homogeneity among the elderly as a group.[93] A rationing program at the macro level predicated on age per se obscures vital individual differences (which are relevant to respective rights) in needs, preferences, and capacities for benefit.[94] Such a policy judges and treats people as labels rather than as autonomous beings. Age should be considered only on the micro level, as one of several rationing factors, and only to the extent that it has predictive value for the particular patient in terms of prognosis and probability of benefit.[95]

Alternatives to Age-Based Rationing

Age-based health-care rationing proposals are objectionable on political, legal, and ethical grounds. Since health-care resources are (or at some point will be) scarce and the existence of an inevitable disparity between demand for health services and ability to satisfy that demand will emerge, what policy alternatives are more palatable?

One possibility is a continuation of the status quo of implicit or soft rationing. Despite its shortcomings, this system has allowed Americans to wink at each other while providing high-quality care to most of our citizens as we maintain a decent level of social tranquillity. As one astute observer of American health care has noted, where nonallocation of resources causes harm or risk of harm, this policy is more likely to be deemed popularly acceptable where the negative consequences are imposed by chance (rather than by choice), indirectly (through omission rather than commission), through latent (rather than overt) decision-making, by an unidentified rationer, and on a rationee who is individually unidentified at the time the risk is created (a statistical life instead of an actual one).[96]

Whichever rationing policy we choose, or fall into, better prospective health planning ought to be more carefully assimilated into standard medical practice for reasons of both patient autonomy and cost containment. Older patients are not anxious to horde expensive but futile or unduly burdensome medical interventions, and many would welcome the opportunity to express their preferences and control their medical futures through living wills and durable powers of attorney. No person should be coerced into executing an advance planning document or forfeiting any medical intervention to which he or she has a right, and certainly not for financial reasons; to the extent, though, that one voluntarily and knowingly elects, as a matter of expressing personal autonomy, to forego particular medical interventions, society should facilitate such an opportunity and accept the cost savings as an incidental but positive by-product.

Another alternative, although not a promising one, is further tinkering with incremental changes in the health-care financing and delivery system of the sort that have destabilized the industry in the past dozen years. The pessimism of Callahan and colleagues on this score is well founded.

Calls for a program of health-care rationing according to age reflect a perception—largely well founded—of a crisis. The most effective and tolerable alternative to age-based rationing may rest with basic, radical reformation of the health-care system, namely, the development of a comprehensive, universal national health insurance program with built-in, integral, tight cost controls based on evidence of a medical service's efficacy. The private medical marketplace is far preferable to a national health service where government delivers as well as subsidizes health care, but a private delivery system where government acts as the single payor or guarantor of payment can and must incorporate tough cost controls (learning to say "no") based on the proven effectiveness and value of an intervention rather than the age or disability per se of the patient. We should not consider explicit rationing except as part of re-forming and building a more just, larger system of health-care delivery, where a fairer and more sensible distribution and use of medical services serves as the quid pro quo for accepting limits on the total volume and mix of services.[97]

Callahan has argued that the elderly are the only group in this nation privileged with a public insurance program (Medicare) regardless of personal ability to pay, and that limiting their privileges is not unfair.[98] If he is correct, the better answer is to entirely abolish Medicare, where eligibility depends on age, and replace it with a universal national health insurance program for everyone. Reasonable limits could then be imposed ethically based on individual capacity for benefit or the type of service, without devaluing any particular group of persons qua group.

Finally, we should not focus discussion purely on questions relating to the distribution of medical benefits. Someone must pay for those benefits that are distributed and rationed, and thoughtful contemplation about the shape of the larger health-care system commands attention to a more equitable distribution of costs. If, as I argue here, the elderly have political, legal, and ethical claims to participate in the benefits of our health-care system on the basis of individual needs, preferences, and capacities for benefit, then there is a correlative social obligation to expand the mandatory resource contributions of those older persons who, judged as individuals, possess the capacity to expand their contributions. Means testing of health-care benefits would open new political and ethical considerations at this time, but even the staunchest of generational equity opponents now concede that a true social insurance scheme—especially one with an effective cost containment component assuring equitable distribution of services—should compel high-income elderly to pay their fair share of the social burden.[99]

Conclusion

Callahan and his supporters have proposed a serious social policy for dealing with a health-care resource scarcity problem that is real and ominous. Both the resource scarcity crisis and the age-based rationing proposals it has generated deserve to be taken seriously. While these proposals are objectionable on political, legal, and ethical grounds, opponents of this approach have an obligation to suggest and help implement social policies of their own that do a better job of promoting social harmony, protecting the legal liberties and entitlements of individuals, and honoring the ethical precepts of autonomy, beneficence, and distributive justice. The concept of health-care rationing by age, in setting up a very thoughtful and difficult target, challenges us all and presents us with an opportunity for creative and honest social policy-making.[100]

NOTES

1. Editorial, "Medicare's Money Pit," *Wall Street Journal,* Jan. 18, 1989, A14, col. 1–2. Between 1967 and 1984, total Medicare expenditures rose from $4.6 billion to $62.9 billion. Gornick, Greenberg, Eggers, and Dobson, "Twenty Years of Medicare and Medicaid: Covered Populations, Use of Benefits, and Program Expenditures," *Health Care Financing Review,* annual supplement (December 1985): 42. In the year 2000, it is estimated that Medicare expenditures will be $320.8 billion. Holahan and Palmer, "Medicare's Fiscal Problems: An Imperative for Reform," 13 *Journal of Health Politics, Policy & Law* 53 (1988).

2. Kapp, "Health Care Tradeoffs Based on Age: Ethically Confronting the 'R' Word," 52 (3) *The Pharos of Alpha Omega Alpha* 2 (Summer 1989).

3. Veatch, "Justice and the Economics of Terminal Illness," 18 *Hastings Center Report* 34, 35 (Aug./Sept. 1988).

4. Reagan, "Health Care Rationing: What Does It Mean?" 319 *New England Journal of Medicine* 1149 (Oct. 27, 1988). For a discussion of the inherent difficulty of identifying waste in health care delivery, see Mehlman, "Health Care Cost Containment and Medical Technology: A Critique of Waste Theory," 36 *Case Western Reserve Law Review* 778 (1985–86); Mehlman, "Age-Based Rationing and Technological Development," 33 (3) *Saint Louis University Law Journal* 671 (Spring 1989). For commentaries on Mehlman's thesis, see Neuhauser, "Medical Technology Assessment as Social Responsibility," 36 *Case Western Reserve Law Review* 878 (1985–86); Perry and Chu, "Health Care Cost Containment and Technology Assessment," 36 *Case Western Reserve Law Review* 884 (1985–86).

5. Ruffenach, "Medical Tests Go Under the Microscope," *Wall Street Journal,* Feb. 7, 1989, B1, col. 4–8; Hornbein, "The Setting of Standards," 256 *Journal of the American Medical Association* 1040 (1986).

6. Furrow, "The Ethics of Cost Containment: Bureaucratic Medicine and the Doctor as Patient-Advocate," 3 (2) *Notre Dame Journal of Law, Ethics and Public Policy* 187, 220–221 (1988).

7. Kapp, " 'Cookbook Medicine': A Legal Perspective," 150 (3) *Archives of Internal Medicine* 496 (1990).

8. One geriatrician has pointed out that it is not usually the older patient who has an insatiable appetite for the use of unlimited technology to preserve life at all costs, but rather the children and caregivers who insist on "doing everything." Olson, "Medical Implications of Setting Limits: Using Age as a Criterion," 33 (3) *Saint Louis University Law Journal* 603, 606 (Spring 1989).

9. Bellamy and Oye, "Admitting Elderly Patients to the ICU: Dilemmas and Solutions," 42 *Geriatrics* 61 (Mar. 1987).

10. Olson, supra note 8, at 607. But see Kapp, "Response to the Living Will Furor: Directives for Maximum Care," 72 (6) *American Journal of Medicine* 855 (1982) (patients should have the option of using advance directives to request more, as well as less, future medical care).

11. Evans, "Age and Equality," in *Biomedical Ethics: An Anglo-American Dialogue* 118, 123–124 (D. Callahan and G. R. Dunstan, eds. 1988), published at 530 *Annals of the New York Academy of Sciences.* See also Olson, supra note 8, at 606.

12. Thomasma, "Moving the Aged into the House of the Dead: A Critique of Ageist Social Policy," 37 *Journal of the American Geriatrics Society* 169, 171 (1989).

13. Kapp, "Enforcing Patient Preferences: Linking Payment for Medical Care to Informed Consent," 261 *Journal of the American Medical Association* 1935 (1989). See also Bierly, "Letter to the Editor," 262 *Journal of the American Medical Association* 1773 (1989) and Kapp, "Response to Letter," 262 *Journal of the American Medical Association* 1774 (1989).

14. *Grace Plaza of Great Neck v. Elbaum,* Index No. 19068/88, Supreme Court, Nassau County (NY), Jan. 9, 1990.

15. Schwartz, "Setting Limits on Autonomy: Saving Money in an Aging Society," 33 (3) *Saint Louis University Law Journal* 617, 625–630 (Spring 1989).

16. Evans, "Health Care Technology and the Inevitability of Resource Allocation and Rationing Decisions, Part 1," 249 *Journal of the American Medical Association* 2047 (1983); "Part 2," 249 *Journal of the American Medical Association* 2208 (1983).

17. Morreim, "Fiscal Scarcity and the Inevitability of Bedside Budget Balancing," 149 (5) *Archives of Internal Medicine* 1012, 1013 (May 1989); Schwartz, "The Inevitable Failure of Current Cost-Containment Strategies," 257 *Journal of the American Medical Association* 220 (1987).

18. Munoz, Rosner, Chalfin, Goldstein, Margolis, and Wise, "Age, Resource Consumption, and Outcome for Medical Patients at an Academic Medical Center," 149 (9) *Archives of Internal Medicine* 1946 (September 1989).

19. Callahan, "Old Age and New Policy," 261 *Journal of the American Medical Association* 905 (1989).

20. Callahan, "Prologue—Health Care for the Elderly: Setting Limits," 33 (3) *Saint Louis University Law Journal* 557, 562 (Spring 1989).

21. Veatch, supra note 3, at 39–40.

22. Daniels, *Am I My Parents' Keeper? An Essay on Justice between the Young and the Old.* New York: Oxford University Press (1988).

23. Eglit, "Health Care Allocation for the Elderly: Age Discrimination by Another Name?" 26 (5) *Houston Law Review* 813, 846 (Oct. 1989); Blumstein, "Age-Based Rationing of Medical Care: A Legal and Policy Critique," 33 (3) *Saint Louis University Law Journal* 693, 700 (Spring 1989).

24. See, e.g., Garland and Buell, "Health Care for All or an Excuse for Cutbacks?" *Business Week,* June 26, 1989, at 68 (describing the state of Oregon's new plan to rank all Medicaid treatments in order of importance, with the state covering only those at the top of the list).

25. Callahan, *Setting Limits: Medical Goals in an Aging Society.* New York: Simon and Schuster (1987); Callahan, "Commentary: Old Age and New Policy," 261 *Journal of the American Medical Association* 905 (1989).

26. Social Security Act, Title 18. See generally, Kinney, "Setting Limits: A Realistic Assignment for the Medicare Program?" 33 (3) *Saint Louis University Law Journal* 631 (Spring 1989).

27. Social Security Act, Title 19.

28. Callahan, "Meeting Needs and Rationing Care," 16 *Law, Medicine & Health Care* 261, 265 (1988).

29. Callahan's ideas on this subject have generated a multiplicity of scholarly responses. See, e.g., Binstock and Post (eds.), *"Too Old" For Health Care? Controversies in Medicine, Law, Economics, and Ethics.* Baltimore: Johns Hopkins University Press (1991); Homer and Holstein (eds.), *A Good Old Age? The Paradox of Setting Limits.* New York: Simon and Schuster (1990).

30. See Aaron and Schwartz, *The Painful Prescription: Rationing Hospital Care.* Washington, D.C.: Brookings Institution (1984); Johnson, "Life, Death, and the Dollar Sign: Medical Ethics and Cost Containment," 252 *Journal of the American Medical Association* 223 (1984).

31. See, e.g., Furrow, "Medical Malpractice and Cost Containment: Tightening

the Screws," 36 *Case Western Reserve Law Review* 985 (1985–86); Morreim, "Commentary: Stratified Scarcity and Unfair Liability," 36 *Case Western Reserve Law Review* 1033 (1985–86). See also Morreim, "Cost Constraints as a Malpractice Defense," 18 *Hastings Center Report* 5 (Feb./Mar. 1988).

32. See Kapp, "Health Care Delivery and the Elderly: Teaching Old Patients New Tricks," 17 *Cumberland Law Review* 437 (1986–87).

33. Silver, "From Baby Doe to Grandpa Doe: The Impact of the Federal Age Discrimination Act on the 'Hidden' Rationing of Medical Care," 37 *Catholic University Law Review* 993, 1063 (Summer 1988).

34. See, e.g., Engelhardt and Rie, "Intensive Care Units, Scarce Resources, and Conflicting Principles of Justice," 255 *Journal of the American Medical Association* 1159 (1986). Compare Morreim, supra note 31, at 1014 (bedside rationing, albeit within broad policy guidelines established by society, is inevitable) to La Puma, Cassel, and Humphrey, "Ethics, Economics, and Endocarditis: The Physician's Role in Resource Allocation," 148 (8) *Archives of Internal Medicine* 1809, 1810 (August 1988) (resource allocation decisions must be made as a social choice, not individually at the bedside); Hiatt, "Protecting the Medical Commons: Who Is Responsible?" 293 *New England Journal of Medicine* 235 (1975) (early call for societal responsibility for health-care allocation decisions). See also Callahan, supra note 20, at 564–565 (bedside rationing will not work, in terms of saving enough money, because of physician recalcitrance).

35. See, e.g., MacIntyre, "The Right to Die Garrulously," in Purtilo (ed.), *Moral Dilemmas: Readings in Ethics and Social Philosophy.* Belmont, Mass.: Wadsworth Publishing Company (1985); MacIntyre, *After Virtue.* Notre Dame, Ind.: Notre Dame University Press (1981), ch. 15; MacIntyre, "Patients as Agents," in Spicker and Engelhardt (eds.), *Philosophical Medical Ethics: Its Nature and Significance.* Dorrecht, Holland: Reidel Publishing Company (1977); Battin, "Age Rationing and the Just Distribution of Health Care: Is There a Duty to Die?" 97 *Ethics* (1987).

36. Neither Callahan nor AGE invented the idea that the elderly should "get out of the way" of the younger generation. Plutarch quotes Euripides as follows: "I hate the men who would prolong their lives / By foods and drinks and charms of magic art / Perverting nature's course to keep off death. / They ought, when they no longer serve the land, / To quit this life, and clear the way for youth."

37. Longman, *Born to Pay: The New Politics of Aging in America* (1987); Preston, "Children and the Elderly: Divergent Paths for America's Dependents," 21 *Demography* 435 (1984). See also Gustaitis, "Old vs. Young in Florida: Preview of an Aging America," 7 *Saturday Review* 12 (1980); Kosterlitz, "Who Will Pay" 18 *National Journal* 570 (1986); Longman, "Taking America to the Cleaners," *Washington Monthly* 24 (Nov. 1982); Longman, "Justice between Generations," 225 *Atlantic Monthly* 73 (1985).

38. Social Security Act, Title 2 (Old Age, Survivors, and Disability Insurance—OASDI).

39. See Callahan, supra note 20, at 561. For a refutation of the "blocking" principle, see Schwartz, supra note 15, at 626 (other groups are swept along the public benefits' coattails of the elderly).

40. Villers Foundation, *On the Other Side of Easy Street: Myths and Facts about the*

Economics of Old Age. Washington, D.C. (1987); Rowland and Lyons, *A Report of the Commonwealth Fund Commission on Elderly People Living Alone: Medicare's Poor, Filling the Gaps in Medical Coverage for Low-Income Elderly Americans.* New York (1987).

41. Clark, "The Social Allocation of Health Care Resources: Ethical Dilemmas in Age-Group Competition," 25 *The Gerontologist* 119, 120 (1985); Kingson, "Generational Equity: An Unexpected Opportunity to Broaden the Politics of Aging," 28 *The Gerontologist* 765, 768–69 (1988).

42. H.R. 2470 (1988), repealed by Consolidated Budget Reconciliation Act of 1989.

43. Kingson, Hirshorn, and Cornman, *Ties That Bind: The Interdependence of Generations.* Potomac, Md.: Seven Locks Press (1986).

44. See, e.g., Binstock and Kahana, review of *Setting Limits: Medical Goals in an Aging Society,* by Daniel Callahan, in 28 *The Gerontologist* 424 (1988).

45. Kapp, "Legal and Ethical Implications of Health Care Reimbursement by Diagnosis Related Groups," 12 *Law, Medicine & Health Care* 245 (1984).

46. Blank, *Rationing Medicine.* New York: Oxford University Press (1988).

47. For Callahan's defense of categorical standards, which he defines as "the employment of visible, objective, universal criteria that can be applied to all (or most) individuals and that do not require complex interpretation to be employed," see Callahan, "Rationing Health Care: Will It Be Necessary? Can It Be Done without Age or Disability Discrimination?" 5 (3) *Issues in Law and Medicine* 353, 354, 359–364 (Winter 1989).

48. On whether the government has a duty in this regard, especially in an age of scarce resources, see Blumstein, supra note 23, at 701; Blumstein, "Financing Uncompensated Care: An Approach to the Issues," 38 (4) *Journal of Legal Education* 511, 513 (Dec. 1988); Jecker, "Disenfranchising the Elderly from Life-Extending Medical Care," 2 (3) *Public Affairs Quarterly* 51, 65–66 (July 1988).

49. See Silver, supra note 33, at 1045–46.

50. Childress, "Ensuring Care, Respect, and Fairness for the Elderly," 14 *Hastings Center Report* 27, 28 (1984).

51. The U.S. Supreme Court has held that beneficiaries have a property interest in Medicare benefits. *O'Bannon v. Town Court Nursing Center,* 447 U.S. 773 (1980). See also *Gray Panthers v. Schweiker,* 652 F.2d 146 (D.C.Cir. 1980).

52. But see Eglit, supra note 23, at 847 (age-based rationing schemes could pass due process muster).

53. Hentoff, "The Pied Piper Returns for the Old Folks," *Human Life Review,* appendix A at 108, 111 (Summer 1988).

54. *O'Connor v. Donaldson,* 422 U.S. 563, 95 S. Ct. 2486, 45 L.Ed.2d 396 (1975) (state could not involuntarily hospitalize person on the grounds of mental illness "without more." The "without more" language has been interpreted to mean "without adequate treatment"); Curran, "The 'Class Action' Approach to Protecting Health-Care Consumers—The Right to Psychiatric Treatment," 286 *New England Journal of Medicine* 26 (1972).

55. *West v. Adkins,* 108 S.Ct. 2250 (1988).

56. See, e.g., *Matthews v. Eldridge,* 424 U.S. 319 (1976); *Goss v. Lopez,* 419 U.S. 565 (1975); *Goldberg v. Kelly,* 397 U.S. 254 (1970).

57. See *Heckler v. Ringer,* 466 U.S. 602 (1984); *Schweiker v. McClure,* 466 U.S. 188 (1982); *United States v. Erika, Inc.,* 456 U.S. 201 (1982).

58. Kinney, supra note 26, at 643–45 (Spring 1989).

59. *U.S. Constitution,* Amendment V; *Bolling v. Sharpe,* 347 U.S. 497 (1954).

60. For a contrary conclusion, holding that such an official rationing program would withstand an Equal Protection challenge, see Blumstein, supra note 23, at 701–4 (Spring 1989); Kinney, supra note 26, at 642–43; Eglit, supra note 23, at 838–60. See also Blumstein, "Rationing Medical Resources: A Constitutional, Legal, and Policy Analysis," 59 *Texas Law Review* 1345 (1981).

61. See Callahan, supra note 47, at 354, 359–62 (advocating the wisdom of categorical standards).

62. Cf. Mariner, "Access to Health Care and Equal Protection of the Law: The Need for a New Heightened Scrutiny," 12 *American Journal of Law and Medicine* 345 (1986) (arguing that traditional equal protection analysis is too rigid and newer rationality review too imprecise to provide just determinations regarding eligibility for health benefits. Mariner concludes that courts should subject claims of unequal protection in the health care context to heightened scrutiny, as health care plays a special role in assuring equality of opportunity). Regarding the role of health care in assuring equality of opportunity, see President's Commission for the Study of Ethical Problems in Medicine and Biomedical and Behavioral Research, *Securing Access to Health Care.* Washington, D.C.: Government Printing Office (1983).

63. *Harris v. McRae,* 448 U.S. 297 (1980); *Poelker v. Doe,* 432 U.S. 519 (1977); *Maher v. Roe,* 432 U.S. 464 (1977). See also *Deshaney v. Winnebago County Department of Social Services,* 109 S.Ct. 998, at 1003: "[O]ur cases have recognized that the Due Process Clauses generally confer no affirmative right to governmental aid, even where such aid may be necessary to secure life, liberty or property interests of which the government itself may not deprive the individual." This passage was quoted with approval in *Webster v. Reproductive Health Services,* 109 U.S. 3040, 3051 (1989).

64. Kinney, supra note 26, at 645–47.

65. *Massachusetts Board of Retirement v. Murgia,* 427 U.S. 307 (1976); *Vance v. Bradley,* 440 U.S. 93 (1979).

66. See Hentoff, supra note 53, at 112; Levine, "Comments on the Constitutional Law of Age Discrimination," 57 *Chi-Kent Law Review* 1081 (1982) (proposing doctrinal development of a constitutional law of age discrimination).

67. See, e.g., *Hunter v. Underwood,* 471 U.S. 222 (1985); *Rogers v. Lodge,* 458 U.S. 613 (1982), *reh'g denied,* 459 U.S. 899 (1982).

68. Somerville, "'Should the Grandparents Die?': Allocation of Medical Resources with an Aging Population," 14 *Law, Medicine & Health Care* 158, 160 (1986).

69. See Callahan, supra note 47, at 363.

70. Blumstein, supra note 23, at 706.

71. Id.

72. *Allgeyer v. Louisiana,* 165 U.S. 578 (1897).

73. See sources cited as supra, note 23.

74. *In re Quinlan,* 355 A.2d 647 (N.J. 1976); *Cruzan v. Director, Missouri Department of Health,* 110 S.Ct. 2841 (1990).

75. See *Harris v. McCrae,* 448 U.S. 297, 100 S.Ct. 2671 (1988); Curran, "The Constitutional Right to Health Care: Denial in the Court," 320 *New England Journal of Medicine* 788 (1989).

76. Haber, "Rationing Is a Reality," 34 *Journal of the American Geriatrics Society* 761 (1986); Strauss, LoGerfo, Yeltatzie, et al., "Rationing of Intensive Care Unit Services: An Everyday Occurrence," 255 *Journal of the American Medical Association* 1143 (1986).

77. Aaron and Schwartz, supra note 30, at 96–97.

78. See Rosenblatt, "Medicaid Primary Care Case Management, the Doctor-Patient Relationship, and the Politics of Privatization," 36 *Case Western Reserve Law Review* 915 (1986).

79. Furrow, supra note 6, at 192–93.

80. Wetle, Cwikel, and Levkoff, "Geriatric Medical Decisions: Factors Influencing Allocation of Scarce Resources and the Decision to Withhold Treatment," 28 *The Gerontologist* 336, 337, 341–42 (1988).

81. Churchill, "Should We Ration Health Care by Age?" 36 *Journal of the American Geriatrics Society* 644, 645 (1988).

82. Callahan, supra note 28, at 261–62.

83. See Silver, supra note 33, at 1072: "As difficult as it may be for Congress to adopt a rationing scheme, the legislature is the most appropriate forum for examining competing concerns and interests, and for formulating a policy which reflects a consensus. If society cannot adopt a rationing policy openly, it should not do so at all."

84. Binstock, "The Aged as Scapegoat," 23 *The Gerontologist* 136 (1983).

85. Reagan, supra note 4.

86. Clark, supra note 41, at 124.

87. Thomasma, supra note 12, at 170.

88. Blumstein, supra note 48, at 523.

89. Callahan, "Aging and the Ends of Medicine," in *Biomedical Ethics: An Anglo-American Dialogue* 125, 128 (D. Callahan and G. R. Dunstan, eds. 1988), published as 530 *Annals of the New York Academy of Sciences.*

90. Thomasma, supra note 12.

91. Crum, "A Pro-Life Response to Daniel Callahan's *Setting Limits,*" 33 (3) *Saint Louis University Law Journal* 611, 614 (Spring 1989).

92. Siegler, "Should Age Be a Criterion in Health Care?" 14 *Hastings Center Report* 24, 25 (1984).

93. See Schneider, "Options to Control the Rising Health Care Costs of Older Americans," 261 *Journal of the American Medical Association* 907 (1989).

94. Russ, "Care of the Older Person: The Ethical Challenge of American Medicine," 4 *Issues in Law and Medicine* 87, 88–89 (1988).

95. Bellamy and Oye, supra note 9.

96. Somerville, supra note 68, at 158.

97. Churchill, supra note 81, at 646–47.

98. Callahan, "Epilogue—Setting Limits: Daniel Callahan Responds," 33 (3) *Saint Louis University Law Journal* 707 (Spring 1989).

99. Kingson, supra note 41, at 770.

100. See generally Kapp, supra note 2.

6

Efficient Allocation of Health Care to the Elderly

LAWRENCE DeBROCK

As front pages of newspapers continue to remind us, public policy toward the aged is a very sensitive and important policy issue. While policy-makers wrangle with the issues of what to do and how to pay for the resulting programs, constant budget pressures have caused many analysts to scour the landscape for relief. Some have called for a reevaluation for our programs for the elderly.[1] Make no mistake about the well-placed motives of these observers. Their attack is not on the elderly per se, but on the size of public expenditures directed to that group. A recent General Accounting Office (GAO) report indicates that the elderly command nearly half of the federal domestic budget and the share is expected to grow over time.[2] The focus of this volume centers on one such proposed program: age-based rationing of health care.

In what follows, I hope to accomplish two goals. First, I want to document the health costs we as a nation face. Callahan (1987) offers his age-based rationing device as a solution to the health-care problem in general. The foundation of his argument is that society cannot afford all we spend on health care, so something (or some group) must cut back. In order to make a more informed judgment about the merits of any rationing proposal, we need to have a better understanding of the state of health-care delivery.

Second, I want to explain and clarify the underlying economics of the problem. Economics is defined as the study of the allocation of scarce resources and is thus aptly suited to consider a proposal for rationing. Do we need to ration? If so, what are the characteristics of a successful rationing scheme?

Much public debate has centered on America's appetite for health-care expenditures. As a nation, we spend more than 12 percent of our income, as measured by gross national product (GNP), on health care. As indicated in Table 1, U.S. spending on health care, measured as a percentage of national income, is significantly higher than in the typical industrialized country. This fact alone is not bothersome; Americans rank number one in

Lawrence DeBrock

many categories of expenditures. The potential for concern arises when one looks at the growth patterns. In the United States the percentage of GNP devoted to health care has continued to grow over time. For example, note that the U.S. percentage was very close to the Canadian rate in 1970 but has grown much more rapidly since that time. The elderly command a disproportionate share of these expenditures on health care. While the elderly comprised only 12 percent of the population in 1987, they spent 36 percent of the health-care dollars.[3]

Table 1. Total Health Expenditures as a Percentage of Gross National Product

	1960	1965	1970	1975	1980	1985	1986	1987
Canada	5.5	6.1	7.2	7.3	7.4	8.4	8.7	8.6
France	4.2	5.2	5.8	6.8	7.6	8.6	8.7	8.6
Germany	4.7	5.1	5.5	7.8	7.9	8.2	8.1	8.2
Japan	2.9	4.3	4.4	5.5	6.4	6.6	6.7	6.8
Sweden	4.7	5.6	7.2	8.0	9.5	9.4	9.1	9.0
United Kingdom	3.9	4.1	4.5	5.5	5.8	6.0	6.1	6.1
United States	5.2	6.0	7.4	8.4	9.2	10.6	10.9	11.2
Mean: OECD[1]	3.8	4.5	5.3	6.5	7.0	7.4	7.3	7.3

Source: Shrieber and Poullier (1989).
1. Organization for Economic Cooperation and Development.

But more than the size of expenditures on health by today's elderly is at issue. A major concern of some advocates of an age-based rationing proposal is the impression that society faces a demographic problem. The United States, as well as the rest of the world, is undergoing an aging of the general population. As medical science has promoted physicians and hospitals from being caretakers of the sick into actual healers, life expectancy rates have continuously risen. The percentage of elderly in our population is higher now than at any point in our history. The longer life brought about by the changing of medical technology combined with the aging of the baby boom segment of the population promises an even older America of tomorrow. Table 2 presents some summary statistics of this aging phenomenon and some forecasts provided by the U.S. Bureau of the Census. We can expect the elderly to grow as a percentage of total population at least through the middle of the next century.

Table 2. U.S. Population Figures and Projections (numbers in thousands)

Year	Total Population	Elderly	Percent Elderly
1960	180760	16675	9.2
1970	205089	20107	9.8
1980	227754	25713	11.3
1990	249657	31697	12.7
2000	267955	34921	13.0
2010	283238	39196	13.8
2020	296597	51422	17.3
2030	304807	64580	21.2
2040	308559	66988	21.7
2050	309448	67412	21.8

Source: *Aging America* (1988)

While this phenomenon has many implications for society, the current focus is on health care. The combination of rapid growth in health-care expenditures in the United States coupled with the changing demographics has led some individuals to conclude that society must intervene in the allocation decisions of the medical marketplace. Proposals for rationing services are not new, and the forms of rationing involve economic and noneconomic criteria.[4] Those calling for intervention, of which Daniel Callahan may be the most obvious, believe that we as a society must make some hard rationing decisions about the use of our limited resources. In that regard, they are 100 percent correct. All goods are subject to the laws of scarcity and therefore *must* be rationed. What can be questioned, however, is the nature of the allocation mechanism suggested. To evaluate fully the soundness of the age-based criterion, all costs, benefits, and implications must be examined.

I present here an introduction and review of the economics involved in this issue, but not as an exercise in normative economics. The reader will not find arguments to the effect "we must spend more (less) on health care for the elderly." Rather, I try to offer factual evidence of what health care costs this country and an assessment of what we can afford. In the process, I will develop some basic understanding of how the health-care market functions. The next section considers the special characteristics of health-care delivery and the historical patterns of market as well as government forces.

Figure 1. Demand and Supply Equilibrium

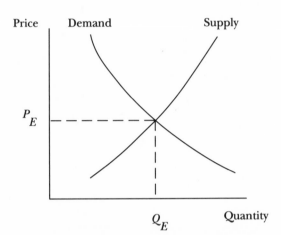

Economics Issues in Health-Care Delivery

Economists are notoriously fond of the market as an allocation tool because it is a very efficient instrument. It forces suppliers to produce in the most sensible fashion (the least cost production technique) for a given output and quality level. It directs scarce resources to those that receive the most value from the activity.

Consider Figure 1, a typical supply and demand curve. Intuitively, the demand curve represents the marginal valuation of consumers for the product in question. For example, pick any arbitrary price that may arise in the market. Read the total quantity consumed from the demand curve at this price. The current interest, however, is society's value of the marginal unit. Consumers placing less value on the good than the price will, of course, stay out of this market. Those that value the good at least as much as this price will purchase the product. The *marginal value* of the product is that value held by those consumers right on the threshold of buying or not buying. Note that we need not identify these precise customers to determine this marginal value. Observation of the price is sufficient, as consumers will rationally self-select into purchasers/non-purchasers according to their own valuation of the product. The price, then, as the rationing device, is an indicator of society's marginal value.

Likewise, *marginal social cost* is reflected by the supply curve. The supply curve represents the value of societal resources used in the production of the marginal units of the good. Typically this curve slopes upward, reflecting that as production of any good increases, resources used in the incremental unit of production become more and more costly.

Finally, we are in a position to understand why a free market equilibrium is so desirable. A free market equilibrium occurs at the price where quantity supplied exactly meets the amount demanded. This point, shown as $P_E Q_E$, has the desirable property that the market clearing price also guarantees that the socially optimal level of activity occurred. The last unit sold contributed a marginal benefit to society exactly equal to the marginal resource cost society incurred in production of that unit. If all works smoothly, the free market price results in the efficient allocation of resources.

Of course, the market does not always function smoothly. In such cases, known as *market failure,* leaving the production, pricing, and allocation decisions to an "invisible hand" generates significant inefficiencies; indeed, perhaps the total absence of a market. The proper response to market failure is enlightened government intervention. Concern by policy-makers over the performance of the health-care market reflects the general perception that one or more characteristics of the market result in some form of market failure. While the list of causes of such market failure is long, the two that receive the most attention are (1) the problem of moral hazard; and (2) the problem of insufficient income.

Moral Hazard

When a population is at risk of a harmful event, but the occurrence of this event is not universal, society has long recognized the advantage of pooling risk. In other eras, when a neighbor's house burned down, farmers would interrupt their own work to provide labor and material to replace the lost structure. Today, we are more than happy to pay insurance companies for the service they provide in finding other individuals to help us share the risk of one of our houses burning down. Loss of health is just one of many things against which we can buy insurance.

Unfortunately, the existence of insurance often leads to a serious inefficiency called moral hazard. Moral hazard refers to situations where the existence of the insurance against some event makes the event more likely to occur. Put differently, if someone else (an insurance company or a government agency) is paying for some event, you are more likely to overconsume.

Consider the health insurance market. Let Figure 1 now represent the demand and supply conditions in the health-care market. If an individual had full coverage insurance, sometimes called "first dollar" coverage, then the price for health care would be zero. Figure 1 shows that the result is excessive consumption of the product. The consumer, facing a price of zero, chooses service at the point where demand eventually hits the horizontal axis. Here, the *last units of health care* do contribute positively to the consumer's well-being. However, the social cost, read off the supply curve, was far more than the benefit received.

It is important not to underestimate the impact of this moral hazard phenomenon. We can argue about the actual shape and position of these curves, but economists have shown repeatedly that the demand curve for health care is negatively sloped and the marginal resource costs are non-zero. The implication should be clear; under the type of insurance coverage in this example, we will see too many resources devoted to health care.[5]

Of course, most health-care insurance has some form of cost-sharing device, usually in the form of a deductible. This "front end payment" indeed makes the consumer think about the decision to purchase a medical service. However, it is not very successful in handling moral hazard problems. To see why, imagine that you were given the role of benevolent dictator of our society. At this very moment you are overseeing the delivery of health care to one of your subjects with such insurance coverage. The fixed deductible is the first amount paid, and quickly the patient's bill is into that portion covered by the insurance company. The physician has an elaborate array of medical services and tests that can be provided to the patient. The first few procedures will be the most beneficial. However, after this initial flurry, subsequent tests will continue to offer less and less *marginal* contribution to the health of the patient.[6] Of course, they do offer some positive value. Neglecting the information asymmetries inherent in this market, does the consumer turn down these extra tests? No, because the marginal value, while low, is above the price the consumer must pay (zero). The physician recognizes the lower and lower value of each successive test but also recognizes that each test provides *some* positive value to the patient. Each test has some probability of being effective and thus the provider sees a positive expected value. The result is an excessive allocation of resources to health care. The benevolent dictator, interested in social efficiency, will recognize the point where the marginal test costs society more than it returns and stop at this level of health care.

Ability to Pay

The second form of market failure in health-care delivery concerns the lack of affordability of minimum health care. Some members of society face income constraints that make adequate health care unattainable, especially in bouts of acute illness. Society has deemed that such a situation is intolerable and intervention is necessary. The existence of major public aid programs such as Medicare demonstrates our belief that a segment of the population, in this case, the elderly, would *underconsume* health care if left entirely to the marketplace. Medicaid, the companion program, offers assistance to those people unable to afford health care, regardless of age. The argument that health care is a public good, not dissimilar to national defense and highways, is the basis for many nations' provision of national health insurance. Such a program has often drawn support from influential sources in the United States. We are, however, exceptional among industrialized nations in our decision not to provide compulsory health care coverage to all members of society.[7] Still, we have made certain commitments suggesting that we believe some minimum level of health care is a right that must be provided regardless of income. These programs reflect the position that some minimum level of health care is a quasi-public good.[8] More will be said on this issue when we move into the material on Medicare and Medicaid.

A Brief History

Unlike property damage insurance, health insurers do not find it practical to send out adjustors to approve claims.[9] Nor has coinsurance (or other devices that make the consumer aware of price) played much of a role. The result has been continued high growth of expenditures on health-care delivery. In response to this artifact of market failure, the government intervened with direct attempts at cost containment. These regulations attacked the supply side of the market by putting direct constraints on the physical inputs to health-care delivery via such restrictions as CON (certificate of need) regulations.[10] Such rules, requiring agency approval of new construction, proved to be of little positive benefit in containing costs.

By the end of the 1970s, the issue of cost containment became more important to the private sector. Statements by automotive executives that health insurance premiums amounted to over $2000 per employee were indicative of the pressure for cost containment brought about by businesses. This demand side movement was the impetus for the growth of CMPs (competitive medical plans). Led most notably by the emerging health maintenance organizations (HMOs), CMPs offered insurance policies that returned some notion of the relative value of the resources to those parties directly involved in the allocation process. As time has passed, insurers have offered an increasing variety of such plans.[11] Each new variety is, of course, meant to offer more attractive benefits to some segment of society; the old plans are still there for those that find them most appealing.

The common principle linking the CMPs is the inherent cost-containment mechanisms. The actual application of pressure on costs comes from one or all participants in the transaction. Some plans force the provider to bear the risk by paying a group of doctors (the HMO providers, for example) a fixed fee regardless of the health-care services that will be eventually supplied. Some plans force the consumer to be more sensitive to costs by strict application of nontrivial copayments, returning to price as a rationing device. Some plans use a third party, the insurance company's management utilization review team, as a device for alerting the two principal decision-makers, the patient and the provider, of the real costs of the health-care procedures. Someone in authority reviews utilization patterns by providers of the health care. Again, such systems vary in nature, but all have the characteristic of making some decision-maker the party at risk. Such systems have been shown to be quite effective in restricting utilization on the margin.[12]

Consider the example of Medicare's prospective payment system (PPS). Faced with extreme cost increases in a time of already severe budgetary pressures, the federal government made a significant policy change in 1983. Using the diagnosis-related group (DRG) classification system, the government determined a fixed price to be paid for a given incidence of medical care according to the most appropriate DRG. If the hospital could provide the service at a cost below the PPS rate, the residual could be kept as profit. If the hospital spent more on the patient than the PPS amount, the excess came from hospital funds. Note the economic significance of this mechanism. The provider is now the party at risk for each resource expended. Allocation decisions will be more efficient as they will be based on marginal values and costs.

PPS has been in place long enough to have produced early signals of its success as a cost-containment device. While the data are not sufficiently rich at a micro level to permit a thorough statistical study, we do have some simple evidence. Figures 2 and 3 offer some confirmation that cost containment is working under the PPS regime instituted in 1983. Figure 2 presents a picture of the percentage change in national health care expenditures.[13] While the general trend line is not dramatic, it is clear that the annual change in health-care expenditures began to slow in the early 1980s. This corresponds with the introduction of PPS for Medicare and the emergence of CMPs in the private insurance market. Even more dramatic evidence of the effect of capitation payments (i.e., PPS) comes from the data on hospital days for the elderly. Figure 3 shows that the number of Medicare hospital days of care per 1,000 aged enrollees dropped precipitously with the introduction of PPS.[14] Again, the cost-containing incentives provided by such a system should be apparent.

Health Care and the Elderly

Before looking more explicitly at health-care expenditures by the elderly, it is worth reemphasizing the main points of the previous section:

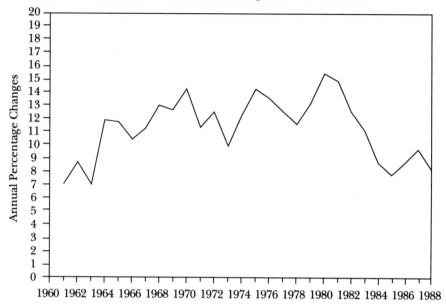

Figure 2. U.S. Health Care Expenditure Growth Rates

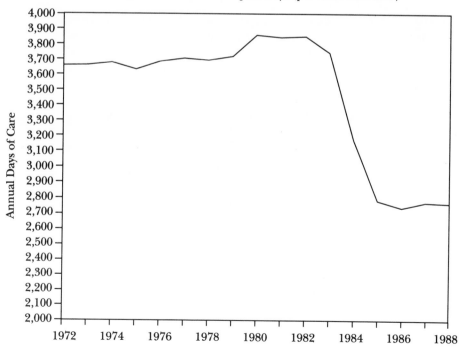

Figure 3. Medicare Hospital Days (per 1,000 Enrollees)

(1) In the absence of market failure, the government and other interveners can trust the market for efficient outcomes.

(2) If neither party involved in the allocation decision is directly at risk, the outcome will be characterized by overconsumption of the product in question.

Put differently, without some belief that market failure has occurred, policy-makers need not concern themselves with the outcomes of the market. The rationing device inherent in the simple supply and demand analysis is not only sufficient, but it is also optimal. However, in health-care delivery, moral hazard problems require attention to the party at risk. Without some reasonable effort at handling this problem, inefficient (and quite costly) levels of health-care expenditures will result.

Current Spending and Sources

As indicated in Figure 2, national health-care expenditures have continued to grow over time. Table 3 presents some statistics that illustrate the growing importance of health-care expenditures in our economy.

In response to the lack of ability to pay, the government has set up programs to help certain classes acquire health care. In addition, we as a society have made certain decisions about health care for the elderly. In 1965 the federal government enacted the Medicare program. Table 3 shows expenditures on Medicare. The experiences of the Medicare and Medicaid programs reflect the general trend in national health care documented above. The last two columns of Table 3 show the percentage of total national income and national health-care expenditures, respectively, devoted to Medicare funds. Medicare has continued to capture a larger share of income and spending until the last few years. Since the imposition of PPS, this growth has slowed; indeed, there has been negative growth relative to national health-care expenditures.

The data in Table 3 indicate the growth of government involvement in the determination of how we as a nation spend our health-care dollars. Figure 4 depicts the pattern of public involvement in the health-care sector, including the rapid growth seen in the second half of the 1960s.[15] While the U.S. public/private share is nowhere near that of other industrialized countries, the government has taken a much more active role since the early 1960s. The growth seems to have tapered off somewhat, but we do not see the more dramatic utilization effects demonstrated in Figure 3. This is partly attributable to the general growth in government involvement in the health-care market and partly because the total number of aged Medicare enrollees has increased.

Table 3. National Income (GNP), Health-Care (HC) Spending,
and Medicare (Mcare)

	Nominal			Real ('82 dollars)			Mcare % of	
Year	GNP	HC	Mcare	GNP	HC	Mcare	GNP	HC
1960	515.3	26.9		1679.5	87.7			
1961	533.8	28.8		1722.3	92.9			
1962	574.4	31.3		1832.9	99.9			
1963	606.9	33.5		1913.4	105.6			
1964	649.8	37.5		2022.1	116.7			
1965	705.1	41.9		2157.1	128.2			
1966	772.0	46.3		2296.1	137.7			
1967	816.4	51.5	3.4	2360.2	148.9	9.8	0.42	6.59
1968	892.7	58.2	5.3	2476.8	161.5	14.8	0.60	9.19
1969	963.9	65.6	6.6	2537.9	172.7	17.4	0.68	10.06
1970	1015.5	75.0	7.1	2524.3	186.4	17.8	0.70	9.53
1971	1102.7	83.5	7.9	2628.1	199.0	18.8	0.71	9.43
1972	1212.8	94.0	8.8	2798.2	216.9	20.4	0.73	9.38
1973	1359.3	103.4	9.5	2952.5	224.6	20.6	0.70	9.17
1974	1472.8	116.1	11.3	2882.8	227.2	22.2	0.77	9.77
1975	1598.4	132.7	14.8	2866.6	238.0	26.5	0.92	11.14
1976	1782.8	150.8	17.7	3022.9	255.7	30.1	1.00	11.77
1977	1990.5	169.9	21.5	3170.5	270.6	34.3	1.08	12.68
1978	2249.7	189.7	25.2	3328.5	280.7	37.3	1.12	13.29
1979	2508.2	214.7	29.1	3335.4	285.5	38.8	1.16	13.58
1980	2731.9	248.1	35.0	3200.1	290.6	41.0	1.28	14.12
1981	3052.6	285.2	42.5	3239.7	302.7	45.1	1.39	14.90
1982	3166.0	321.2	50.4	3166.0	321.2	50.4	1.59	15.70
1983	3405.7	357.2	56.9	3299.6	346.1	55.1	1.67	15.92
1984	3772.2	388.5	62.7	3505.4	361.0	58.3	1.66	16.14
1985	4014.9	419.0	72.3	3602.4	376.0	64.9	1.80	17.26
1986	4240.3	455.7	77.7	3732.9	401.2	68.4	1.83	17.05
1987	4526.7	500.3	80.8	3844.5	424.9	68.6	1.78	16.15

Source: Ginsburg (1988); Helbing and Keene (1988). 1987 figures for Medicare are estimates.

As large as the numbers in Table 3 are, it is still true that the elderly pay as out-of-pocket expenses a sizable percentage of their health-care expenditures. Table 4 gives a simple percentage breakdown of the source of the spending on health care for the elderly.[16]

One very significant point that the data do not reveal is that much of the spending for long-term care is not even reported. Meltzer (1988) estimates that as much as 80 percent of long-term care services is provided without charge. These services represent aid by family, friends, and volunteer caregivers.

The growth in Medicare spending reflects that fact that its target population, the elderly, is the segment of the population that is the heaviest users of health care. Although such age-group expenditure data are not widely available, those careful studies of national health-care expenditures that do exist suggest a clear pattern. In 1987 the elderly consumed over one-third of our national health-care expenditures while comprising only 12 percent of the population.[17] Elderly patients consumed 36 percent of the health care in 1987 as compared with only 30 percent in 1977. Of course, part of the increase in health-care expenditures by the elderly is a natural consequence of their increasing importance in the demographic profile. The elderly population growth rate of that period was significant, moving from 10.8 percent to 12.4 percent of the total population.[18] To determine if elderly are increasing their share relative to other groups, it is necessary to standardize by population density.

Figure 4. Government Funding of Health Care

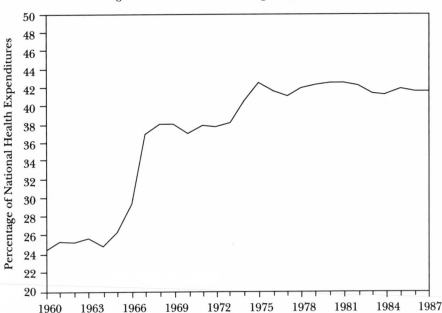

Table 4. Per Capita Elderly Personal Health Care Expenditures,
by Source of Funds, 1984

Payment Source	Per Capita Expenditures	Percent of Total Expenditures	Shares of Category Spending			
			Hospital	Physician	Nursing Home	Other
Private						
Out-of-Pocket	1059	25	5.6	21.4	33.1	31.3
Insurance	304	7	49.2	38.6	3.3	8.9
Government						
Medicare	2051	49	59.7	18.6	15.0	6.8
Medicaid	536	13	17.0	3.1	68.1	11.8
Other	236	6	73.2	2.4	16.5	7.9

Source: *Aging America* (1988).

Table 5 gives such indication by presenting per capita spending levels. To control for inflation, Table 5 presents three sets of numbers. The first group represents nominal (current) dollar consumption. The second group deflates by the standard CPI (consumer price index) deflator in an attempt to obtain real spending levels. The third group adjusts

Table 5. Real Per Capita Annual Health Expenditures by Age Group

	All ages	Under 20	20–64	65 and older
Nominal current dollars				
1977	658	269	651	1856
1987	1776	745	1535	5360
Real (CPI adjusted; '82 dollars)				
1977	1048	428	1037	2955
1987	2883	1209	2492	8701
Real (Medical CPI adjusted; '82 dollars)				
1977	559	229	553	1577
1987	1263	530	1092	3812

Source: Waldo, Sonnefeld, McKusick and Arnett (1989).

for the growth in costs of medical care alone. The middle tier, then, shows spending levels deflated on the basis of economy-wide inflation rates. The third group more accurately reflects real per capita health-care consumption as it controls for inflation specific to the health care sector.

It is clear that the aged are spending an ever-increasing share of the health dollar. When these per capita figures are compared with the growth in the total number of elderly, the health-care expenditures of the elderly sector become even more important. Forecasting expenditures is too imprecise and thus of no use to us in this matter. However, it is clear that the percentage of our population that falls into the "elderly" classification will continue to grow. This demographic phenomenon will have a significant impact on national health-care expenditures. Regardless of the demographics, Table 5 shows that the health-care spending per elderly is growing faster than such expenditures in other age groups. If this trend continues, the growth in costs for health care for the elderly will be even more significant.

The implications of Figure 3 do temper this forecast. If the recent introduction of PPS is indeed having a permanent impact on levels and rates of spending, the estimated growth rates (and forecasts) may overstate the health-care expenditures of the elderly. However, there are also indications of a possible source of serious underestimation. There is a potentially dramatic effect on health care for the elderly that could arise through an increase in coverage with respect to nursing home care. Currently, a patient in a nursing home faces costs of about $20,000 to $30,000 annually.[19] Nationally, we spent over $32 billion on nursing homes in 1988, and the forecast is for spending in 2018 to exceed $98 billion (all values in 1982 dollars).[20] Economic analyses of price elasticity of demand suggest substantial quantity responsiveness to price changes in the nursing home segment. If society decides to "pick up the tab" for the spending, it is imperative that such a program be well planned and cognizant of the moral hazard problem. As the earlier section indicated, efficient outcomes will only come when the parties involved face the proper incentives.

The recent reaction by the elderly in response to the Medicare Catastrophic Coverage Act of 1988 is instructive.[21] The movement to repeal the act indicates the sensitivity of the payment issue. This political sensitivity is overshadowed by clear economic ramifications. If the direct consumers of the health care are able to avoid being at risk for the medical services they use, some other control must be imposed on the market.

Figure 5. Support Ratios (Dependent Population per Working-Age Population)

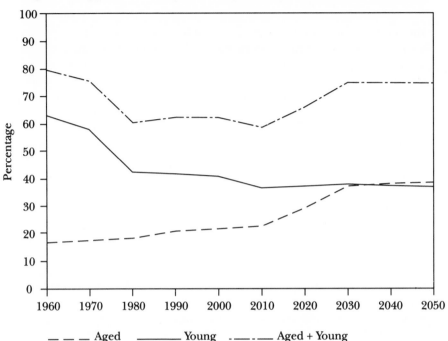

_ _ _ Aged ——— Young . _ . _ Aged + Young

Can We Afford to Pay for Health Care?

This question is meant to be rhetorical. I have tried to present the reader with an understanding of the background statistics, a look at the projections, and, most importantly, a view at the underlying economics. As long as effective controls that solve the moral hazard problem are in place, society will continue to purchase more health care, and *this growth in health care will be optimal.*

Still, many argue that the ever-growing elderly population will prove to be a serious drain on the working population. This argument is founded in the idea that "pay as you go" public aid programs require a sufficiently large working population to support the dependent class.[22] Examination of these statements requires construction of a data series called the support ratio. The support ratio is defined as the ratio of the size of the dependent population to the size of the working class. Figure 5 depicts this ratio for the time period 1960 through 2050. The projected increase in importance of the aged population causes their support ratio to increase over time.

However, any examination of what society can afford must look at the ratio of dependents to workers. The baby boom blip that is moving through the demographic charts is, by definition, moving out of the "young" on its way to the "old." With that in mind, Figure 5 also traces the support ratio for the young, a number declining over time. The sum of these two support ratios, the total amount of dependent population to be supported by the working population, is projected to decline until the early 2010s whereupon it will start climbing again. However, the projected population cohorts predict that by the year 2050 society's total support ratio will not reach the level it attained in the 1960s.

Figure 5 gives the impression that society will have the resources to support its dependent population. However, there are two caveats. First, as shown earlier (Table 5) the amount of health-care expenditures for the elderly are significantly higher than those for the young. As the elderly share of the dependent population rises, the working population will have an increasing financial burden. Second, most of the expenditures on the dependent class called the young are private expenditures. Table 4 shows that public money is the most common source of funding for the aged. Pressure for this share will increase as the political power of the aged grows with its population weight. The declining support ratio shows that we will have the productive capacity to sustain the growing elder population. However, society must be convinced to transfer private funds, formerly spent on dependent children, to the government for use in ever-larger public assistance programs.

Financing Long-Term Care

As the expenditures on health care for the elderly continue to grow, it is clear that some plans for funding must be developed. The Medicare Catastrophic Coverage Act of 1988, while covering only acute illnesses, also brought increased public attention to the burden of nursing home costs. Both of these sources of health-care spending by the elderly can be expected to continue to grow.

Of course, the public could just match the growth in health care for the elderly with increasing funds from the general revenue. This is not a very promising scenario. At the outset, the overwhelming budget constraints faced by legislators renders such a plan doubtful. The recent move to repeal the Medicare Catastrophic Coverage Act of 1988 depicts this well. Lawmakers want to help the elderly, but they will abandon their plans if the only option is to put further strain on the budget deficit.

More funding for the elderly's health-care expenditures will have to come from private sources (Figure 5).[23] Many options have been suggested.[24] Although I cannot here undertake an in-depth analysis of these proposals, I do want to mention a few of the more promising ones.

. First, and most obvious, is insurance. While private insurance for long-term care has been noticeably lacking, there has been a recent increase in the private insurer interest. Burke (1988) reports that as late as 1986 there were no individual long-term care policies available. In 1987 there were only four, but by 1988 there were over seventy. Wallack (1988) offers a compelling argument that long-term care is an area quite suited to insurance. Since 57 percent of the elderly will never enter a nursing home, and 80 percent will spend less than three months in a nursing home, the population has the characteristics necessary to make risk pooling (i.e., insurance) work.[25]

Such insurance coverage can take a variety of forms. Besides the traditional indemnity style insurance, public and private sector organizations have been experimenting with several new plans. One type, called the social health maintenance organization (S/HMO) acts much like a traditional HMO, consolidating both long-term and acute care for elderly. Another form, the continuing care retirement community (CCRC), provides a complete living environment for elderly, including health-care services. Meiners (1988) and Lewin and Wallack (1989) offer excellent reviews of the early experiences under these programs.

Long-term care is a known risk and should be anticipated. However, some mechanism for cash accumulation or prefunding must be devised. One form of private funding could come in the form of long-term care IRAs or other savings plans. Moran and Weingart (1988) offer several suggestions for changes in the tax policy that would increase incentives to accumulate funds for long-term care.[26]

Matching the pattern of health-care expenditures with funding also can be accommodated via some form of home equity conversion.[27] Many authors have advocated the use of reverse annuity mortgages (RAM). These programs offer homeowners the right to annuities as they effectively "sell" back their house. Since over 75 percent of the elderly own their own homes, this could be a very useful vehicle to pay for insurance premiums or copayments.[28] To date, such financial vehicles have been very rarely used. However, in an interesting review of the status of RAMs, Weinrobe (1988) expresses optimism for growth of this funding approach.

Before closing, it is important to stress the fragility of these forecasts. Several studies have demonstrated that the demand for nursing home services is very price elastic.[29] We have already documented that over 80 percent of the long-term care services for elderly are provided without charge. Researchers report that elderly are nearly unanimous in their desire to stay out of nursing homes. However, if outside aid increases, it seems likely that fewer families will bear the burden privately.

Conclusion

The United States has high quality health care, and we spend a large amount for this service. Many argue that we spend too much on health care. We have demonstrated the real possibility of overspending due to moral hazard. Recent trends toward cost containment promise more efficient outcomes.

Our future spending patterns will undoubtedly grow. This growth will not just be a result of increasing population. Rather, much of the growth will come because we will be getting richer. Wealthier people buy an increasingly larger amount of health care. Microeconomic models that provide theoretical justification of the logic behind such a prediction are numerous. Table 6 documents the level of income elasticity for health-care services across nations. The term income elasticity is formally defined as the percentage change in consumption brought about by a one percent change in income. It measures responsiveness of health-care expenditures to changing standards of living. As is obvious, health care is a very income elastic good. As nations grow more wealthy, they devote a larger percentage of their budgets to health. The table suggests that the health-care sector will become an ever-increasing portion of GNP across international boundaries.

Table 6. Income Elasticity of Real Health Care Expenditures
to Gross National Product

	1960–75	1975–84	1960–84
Canada	1.6	1.3	1.5
France	1.6	2.6	1.9
Germany	1.2	0.9	1.3
Japan	1.3	1.6	1.4
Sweden	2.4	1.6	2.7
United Kingdom	2.1	1.0	2.1
United States	1.8	1.2	1.7
Mean: OECD nations	1.6	1.3	1.6

Source: Shrieber and Poullier (1989).

Callahan and others take the position that health care markets are somehow tight and that we are going to have to make hard decisions about rationing to be able to provide a minimum level of health care. Table 6 is a reminder that while the resources devoted to health care are certain to continue to rise, this increase is a natural outcome. It is a reflection of consumer preferences and incomes, as is true of other sectors of spending.[30]

There is nothing special about spending 12 percent of our national income on health care. Given our income elasticity, we can expect national health-care expenditures to be over 15 percent of GNP by the turn of the century. Again, this is not a matter of concern; there is no critical threshold level, no magic percentage limit on health-care expenditures.

This is not the place to put on rose-colored glasses, however. Just as it is clear that health-care expenditures will become an increasing part of our budgets, it is also clear that a solution to the moral hazard problem must be forthcoming. As society takes on more responsibility for the health-care obligations of the elderly, such expenditures could become socially inefficient. The scale of these inefficiencies could indeed be enormous.[31]

What Callahan and his supporters have correctly perceived is the need for *some* policy intervention in the rationing of health care. Society has deemed health care to be, in some sense, a merit good: a privilege owed to everyone in our society. However, in handling the process of making this care available to those not able to access it by their own means, we must be careful to avoid exacerbating the moral hazard problems. Some decision-maker in the allocation process must understand the true resource costs of the health-care procedure in question: some decision-maker must be made the party at risk.

I have tried to make it clear that the question of "resource availability" is wrong-headed. We as a society will have a continually increasing appetite for health-care services. The interesting question is not whether this increase in demand for health care is bad or good. Rather, the question is how to guarantee that the allocation mechanism is both equitable and efficient.

If we were able to solve the moral hazard problem while setting up our social aid programs, we would have no reason to be concerned about the size of health-care expenditures. Consider this simple analogy. We as a society have an ever-increasing appetite for leisure activity. Such expenditures are income elastic; we use them at a greater rate as we get richer. No one is calling for government intervention to ration this industry as its spending takes up more and more of our national income. Why? Because this is a market that "works." The health-care market has demonstrated well-established market failures, and policy-makers have intervened. If we operated these regulatory programs "perfectly," market failures would be mitigated and the outcome would approach the efficient solution. Conversely, a poorly devised intervention scheme results in even more inefficiency than does an unchecked market failure.

Callahan's proposed age-based rule has only one attraction: it is one of the simplest rationing rules one could follow. The other contributors to this volume have pointed out noticeable flaws in such a rationing scheme. From an economic standpoint, it should be clear that some form of rationing of resources *is* a necessity. This is the case in all markets. Regardless of the ethical, moral, and constitutional issues involved with age-based rationing, such a rationing rule has nothing to do with efficiency. Rather than attempt to make decision-makers more aware of the real cost of resources used, such a program would try to limit health care by fiat, by strict application of an arbitrary threshold.

The future will involve hard policy decisions. The recent repeal of the Medicare Catastrophic Coverage Act of 1988 made it clear that the parties involved are all too aware of the question of "who will pay?" for society's stated obligation to help all citizens afford some minimal level of health care. I have tried to convey the message that the rationing scheme should be centered on efficiency. The key to efficiency lies in making certain that those in a position of deciding care levels—providers, patients, and insurers—have the proper incentives. That is, these allocation makers should be aware that health-care resources are limited and do involve real social cost. Balancing such social costs with social benefits should be the goal of the intervention mechanism, not some single-minded goal of reducing expenditures by simply lopping off one tail of the distribution of users.

NOTES

1. For purposes of this paper, the term elderly will be used interchangeably with the term aged; both terms refer to people sixty-five years of age and older.

2. *An Aging Society,* 2.

3. Waldo, Sonnefeld, McKusick, and Arnett, 1989.

4. See, for example, Evans (1983) and Strauss et al. (1986).

5. One might legitimately ask why other types of insurance markets are less susceptible to moral hazard. In fact, they are subject to the same incentives. However, they have successfully implemented cost-sharing devices (deductibles) or review procedures (two estimates before authorizing repair) that greatly mitigate the moral hazard. Additionally, the event insured against, as well as the remedy, are more readily observable than the typical health-care episode.

6. Exactly how soon this point of diminishing marginal returns sets in is not important to this argument. All that is needed is the recognition that as the physician gets further and further into the array of possible tests and procedures, the *marginal* impact on the patient's health gets smaller and smaller.

7. This situation may not be long lived. The New York *Times* reported (Sept. 24, 1989) that the editor of the *New England Journal of Medicine* stated that he would "be willing to bet" that we would have some form of national health insurance "by the end of the century."

8. A public good is usually defined as a one whose benefits are not depleted when a member of society uses the good in question (e.g., national defense). Health care is a good that provides spillover benefits to the rest of society, but the use of health care by the patient does indeed deplete resources, hence the name, quasi-public goods.

9. Of course, requirements such as preadmission authorization and concurrent review are the analogous devices in health care markets.

10. For an excellent review of this, see Temin (1988).

11. At the time of this writing, the fastest growing segment of this market is the preferred provider organization.

12. As should be obvious, the restriction in utilization might have implications for quality of care. Economists argue that providers have the proper incentive to offer the correct level of care for at least two reasons. First, the majority of consumers have alternative choices among health care packages, and second, the very real threat of malpractice litigation forces providers to pay close attention to proper procedures.

13. Data for Figure 2 come from Kowalczyk, Freeland, and Levit (1988).

14. Data for Figure 3 come from Latta and Keene (1990) and represent short-stay hospital inpatient services.

15. Data for Figure 4 come from Letsch, Levit, and Waldo (1988).

16. Note: Out-of-pocket payments in Table 4 do not include private insurance premiums or premium payments for Medicare Part B.

17. Waldo, Sonnefeld, McKusick, and Arnett (1989).

18. 23.9 million to 30.2 million, a real rate of growth of 2.37 percent while the U.S. population in general grew at a rate of 1.02 percent.

19. Moon and Smeeding (1989), 148.

20. Rivlin and Wiener (1988), 11.

21. Of course, it is unclear whether the majority of elderly went along with their lobbying representatives in this particular case.

22. Readers may recall the late 1970s–early 1980s predictions of bankruptcy for the Social Security fund. These arguments were likewise founded on the idea that the relative size of the working population was diminishing.

23. Again, one such route is the indirect path of increasing taxes and using this revenue to pay for public aid programs. While such a scenario may be more palatable in the future, no contemporary political party has had success with programs involving increased taxes.

24. The list of sources on this topic is quite extensive. However, perhaps the most comprehensive and thoughtful treatments can be found in Rivlin and Weiner (1988) and Lewin and Wallack (1989).

25. Gruenberg, Tompkins, and Porell (1989). This study also determined that 85 percent of all people reaching sixty-five years of age will have just *one* expected hospitalization over an eight-year period.

26. Hendrickson (1988) considers the effects of state tax initiatives on long-term care provision.

27. Current Medicaid eligibility rules require that elderly spend down some of their assets before aid is given.

28. *Aging America* (1988). The total equity of these homes amounts to over $550 billion.

29. Neyman (1989) found price elasticity of −1.7 and income elasticity of 1.2; both indicate that future use of nursing home will increase faster than the projections. Scanlon (1980) and Chiswick (1976) found price elasticities of −1.1 and −2.3, respectively.

30. As a point of reference, various studies have estimated the income elasticity for automobiles to be greater than 3.0 while that of owner-occupied housing is greater than 1.5.

31. In fact, many of the doomsday scenarios used as evidence to support radical rationing programs are not caused by demographics or technology but are just prime examples of moral hazard. This moral hazard and the spending problems it generates would exist even if our elderly population was not on the growth path we foresee.

REFERENCES

Aging America, U.S. Senate Special Committee on Aging, 1988.

An Aging Society, U.S. General Accounting Office, September 1986, GAO/HRD-86-135.

Burke, Thomas, "Long-Term Care: The Public Role and Private Initiatives," *Health Care Financing Review,* 1988 Annual Supplement, 1–6.

Callahan, Daniel, *Setting Limits: Medical Goals in an Aging Society.* New York: Simon and Schuster, 1987.

Chiswick, Barry, "The Demand for Nursing Home Care: An Analysis of the Substitution between Institutional and Non-Institutional Care," *Journal of Human Resources* 11 (1976): 295–316.

Evans, R., "Health Care Technology and the Inevitability of Resource Allocation and Rationing Decisions," Parts I and II, *Journal of the American Medical Association* 249 (1983): 2047–53, 2208–19.

Ginsburg, Paul B., "Public Insurance Programs: Medicare and Medicaid," in *Health Care in America,* ed. H. E. Frech. San Francisco: Pacific Research Institute, 1988.

Gruenberg, L., C. Tompkins, and F. Porell, "The Health Status and Utilization Patterns of the Elderly: Implications for Setting Medicare Risk-Based Payments," in *Advances in Health Economics and Health Services Research,* vol. 10, ed. R. Scheffler and L. Rossiter. Greenwich, Conn.: JAI Press, 1989, 41–74.

Helbing, Charles, and Roger Keene, "Use and Cost of Physician and Supplier Services Under Medicare, 1986," *Health Care Financing Review* 10 (Spring 1989): 109–22.

Hendrickson, Michael, "State Tax Incentives for Persons Giving Informal Care to the Elderly," *Health Care Financing Review,* 1988 Annual Supplement, 123–28.

Kowalczyk, George I., Mark S. Freeland, and Katharine R. Levit, "Using Marginal Analysis to Evaluate Health Spending Trends," *Health Care Financing Review* 10 (Winter 1988): 123–29.

Latta, Viola B., and Roger Keene, "Use and Cost of Short-Stay Hospital Inpatient Services under Medicare," *Health Care Financing Review* 12 (Fall 1990): 91–99.

Letsch, Suzanne, Katherine Levit, and Daniel Waldo, "National Health Expenditures, 1987," *Health Care Financing Review* 10 (Winter 1988): 109–22.

Lewin, Marion, and Stanley Wallack, "Strategies for Financing Long-Term Care," in *The Care of Tomorrow's Elderly*, ed. M. Lewin and S. Sullivan. Washington, D.C., American Enterprise Institute, 1989, 161–76.

Meiners, Mark, "Reforming Long-Term Care Financing through Insurance," *Health Care Financing Review*, 1988 Annual Supplement, 109–12.

Meltzer, Judith, "Financing Long-Term Care: A Major Obstacle to Reform," in *The Economics of Long-Term Care and Disability*, ed. S. Sullivan and M. Lewin. Washington, D.C.: American Enterprise Institute, 1988, 56–72.

Moon, Marilyn, and Timothy Smeeding, "Can the Elderly Afford Long-Term Care?," in *The Care of Tomorrow's Elderly*, ed. M. Lewin and S. Sullivan. Washington, D.C.: American Enterprise Institute, 1989, 137–60.

Moran, Donald, and Janet Weingart, "Long-Term Care Financing through Federal Tax Incentives," *Health Care Financing Review*, 1988 Annual Supplement, 117–21.

Neyman, J. A., "The Private Demand for Nursing Home Care," *Journal of Health Economics* 8 (June 1989): 209–31.

Rivlin, Alice, and Joshua Wiener, *Caring for the Disabled Elderly: Who Will Pay?* Washington, D.C.: The Brookings Institution, 1988.

Scanlon, William, "A Theory of the Nursing Home Market," *Inquiry* 17 (1980): 25–41.

Schulz, James, *The Economics of Aging*, 4th ed. Dover, Mass.: Auburn House, 1988.

Shrieber, George, and Jean-Pierre Poullier, "International Health Care Expenditure Trends, 1987," *Health Affairs* 8 (Fall 1989): 169–77.

Strauss, M. et al., "Rationing of Intensive Care Unit Services. An Everyday Occurrence," *Journal of the American Medical Association* 255 (1986): 1143–46.

Temin, Peter, "An Economic History of American Hospitals," in *Health Care in America*, ed. H. E. Frech. San Francisco: Pacific Research Institute, 1988, 75–102.

Waldo, Daniel, Sally Sonnefeld, David McKusick, and Ross Arnett, "Health Care Expenditures by Group, 1977 and 1987," *Health Care Financing Review* 10 (Summer 1989): 111–20.

Wallack, Stanley, "Recent Trends in Financing Long-Term Care," *Health Care Financing Review*, 1988 Annual Supplement, 97–102.

Weinrobe, Maurice, "Home Equity Conversion and the Financing of Long-Term Care," *Health Care Financing Review*, 1988 Annual Supplement, 113–15.

Epilogue
Will the Real Daniel Callahan
Please Stand Up?

ROBERT L. BARRY, O.P., AND GERARD V. BRADLEY

Since the appearance of *Setting Limits,* Daniel Callahan has published another work, *What Kind of Life,* which argues for setting clear and firm limits on the allocation of care and treatments, particularly those aimed at the elderly. In this later work he calls for strict prohibitions on providing curative treatments for the elderly and for curbs on research into cures of diseases of the elderly. In it he strikes at the root of American culture.

Callahan argues that the American health-care system must change. He favors rigid and objective standards for rationing because these would bring the greatest savings. In addition, they can be objectively inspected, evaluated, and debated, unlike more subjective standards. Softer standards would not reduce spending, even though he would consider them to be in accord with the norms of justice, equity, and fair play. However, these standards would be wholly unacceptable and unfair when applied to the elderly. But if this is the case, then why does he permit their application with selected groups such as the handicapped, and why is there debate if the only option is to adopt his hard proposal?

Callahan argues that three forces have created the current crisis in health care: "a broad, limitless definition of health; a highly subjective notion of individual need, one captivated by the diversity of personal goals and desires, and a strong view of human rights, in particular the right of individuals to have access to adequate health care." He denies that a health-care system should be hostage to the individual needs of persons, and, therefore, it should have no obligation to provide cure to those who have lived beyond their natural lifespan. He wants to wean our society away from the unlimited pursuit of individual cures, even though this is probably what most people desire.[1] He would create a situation in which the elderly could find no cures for the diseases that afflict them and in which achieving cures for others would become increasingly problematic.

Callahan's image of society is, nonetheless, one in which wisdom and maturity prevail and that has hopes and dreams tempered, but not abolished or eliminated, by maturity and wisdom. This is a good image, but it is tainted by the complete exclusion of the elderly. He fails to see that one needs to have truly wise and mature persons in a wise and mature society, and one wonders why they alone should be denied all curative medical treatments.

His aim is to achieve "implosion" of the health-care system and reverse its "explosion."[2] These terms are alluring, but he seems to be more interested in achieving reversal of growth and demand rather than anything as techno-sexy as implosion. This can be accomplished by deemphasizing the need to find a cure for all our ailments and by substituting care for cures.[3] He denies that a perfect correlation exists between health and happiness or between the common good and health. There need to be curbs on choices and demands by the aged. Most important, Callahan posits in *Setting Limits* that curing should cease after one reaches the end of a biographical lifespan.[4] Caring beyond that span is all that a sensible public policy should allow.

For Callahan, health-care aspirations are reasonable if they include a desire for full lifespan, fulfillment of cognitive, emotional, and functional needs, rehabilitation, and vocational therapy and nothing more. The primary cause of our inflated expenditures for health care is our desire to expand choice and improve quality without limit; curbing that desire is more difficult and more necessary than rationing. To decrease health-care expenditures, we have to limit our aspirations and demands for health care. Callahan believes that far too much money is being spent on health care, and he contrasts the increasing improvement of American health care to the dilapidated condition of American schools.[5]

Why, we might ask Callahan, is it excessive to desire a full biological lifespan, particularly when this can be gained by moderate personal expenditure? If the desire of the elderly to live a full biological lifespan is irrational, would the desire of a handicapped person to live such a life be rational, even though it could be far costlier to support than it would to support that of an elderly person? Callahan's proposal would meet the curative needs of virtually all categories of patients except the elderly.[6] Loosely speaking, the lifespans of disabled persons are being unnaturally extended by rehabilitation, at least partially, and they have no more right to life-extending, expensive, curative measures than do the elderly.

Callahan divides care and treatment into three types and proposes a pyramid of care levels. At the bottom is "level one care," which includes nutrition, sanitary care, immunization, nursing home care, accident prevention, prenatal care, routine diagnosis and therapy, and emergency medicine.[7] But there is a large hole in the bottom of the pyramid where the least expensive and most efficacious care is given, for the elderly are totally denied that form of care. The second level involves curative treatment of remediable conditions that are effective over the long term. At the top is the class of experimental and technologically sophisticated treatments with little or unknown prospects for success. At this level he calls for more restraint in the demands made by the public.

Callahan calls for the establishment of priorities in providing curative treatments. To have a right to care or treatment, one must meet certain standards, and the most important one is what he calls "health symmetry," which holds that a life-sustaining measure must balance curing against quality of life.[8] Because of the rapid growth of highly sophisticated medical technology, Callahan believes we must evaluate medical technology prior to its implementation. Only those technologies that provide long-term overall outcomes at the lowest overall general cost should be pursued.[9] One difficulty with this principle is that he does not define the material conditions that constitute an acceptable quality of life, leaving the reader to postulate these conditions. A standard that holds that medical treatment is not to be given if it cannot promote long-term recovery could bode ill for the elderly, given Callahan's refusal to countenance public expenditures for curative treatments for this class of people.[10] The only hard and fast, concrete, categorical proposal that *might* bring a reduction of expenditures is the proposal to curb expenditures for the elderly, which he first made in *Setting Limits*.

There are a number of features of this new book that are not only quite troubling, but which also appear to contradict the central claims of *Setting Limits*, which will be discussed next.

Totalitarian Medical Care

Lest one think that Callahan has abandoned his age-based rationing proposal in *What Kind of Life,* be assured that it has been given new life and shape. He does not back away from a central claim of *Setting Limits*—that no person who has lived beyond his or her natural lifespan should be given medical treatments from public funds. In *What Kind of Life* he modifies his proposal, however, by permitting such a person to procure health care privately, even though this violates the principles of equity and fairness articulated in *Setting Limits. What Kind of Life* also goes further than *Setting Limits* in calling for massive federal and state education programs to persuade the public of the benefits and merits of his proposals.

What Kind of Life is in conflict with itself in many areas. For example, Callahan demands minimal levels of cure and care, but he denies these to the elderly.[11] He believes that everyone should get a fair, but smaller, share of the pie, but again excludes the elderly. He clearly says that there should be firm limits against the use of public funds for curative treatments for the elderly, but he would permit them to use private funds to procure desired treatments. In *Setting Limits,* he denied the elderly nursing care because this was one of the costliest aspects of care, but he seems to have backed away from this proposal in *What Kind of Life.* [12] But even this is not entirely clear, however, for he argues vigorously in *What Kind of Life* that firm limits on providing care and cures for the elderly must be maintained to achieve real reductions in health-care expenditures.

The totalitarian character of Callahan's thought remains. *What Kind of Life* refuses to allow one to opt out of the categorical ban against giving curative treatment to the elderly for reasons of conscience. This totalitarianism is obscured by his concession for pragmatic necessity. We cannot impose limits immediately and without qualification, but we must move toward that objective because it is the only practically workable solution. [13]

In *Setting Limits* Callahan spoke at length of the obligations imposed by the requirements of intergenerational equity, and he viewed these as imposing an obligation to refrain from incurring such high expenses for health care that future generations would be impoverished. But no mention is made of those obligations in *What Kind of Life,* which is surprising, for the duties of intergenerational equity played a crucial part in justifying age-based rationing in *Setting Limits,* and yet no consideration was given them in his second book. [14] But if these obligations to future generations still remain in *What Kind of Life,* there is a difficult judgment to be made: would it really be better to leave future generations a debt-free legacy with a retarded medical technology, or would it be better to leave them one of debt with continuing advances in medical technology? With little doubt there should be a duty to future generations to continue advancing research against Alzheimer's, cancer, sexually transmitted diseases, Parkinson's, stroke, and heart attack, but Callahan does not discuss this point in either book. He seems less interested in leaving future generations a legacy of diminished research, technology, therapy, and total medical neglect of the elderly than in leaving them debt-free. If such an obligation exists, it would appear to impose a duty to continue substantial outlays in medical research and care to advance the treatment of these conditions.

Medical Pessimism

In *What Kind of Life* Callahan takes a very dim view of contemporary medicine, seeing it as consuming massive amounts of resources and bringing little benefit. He claims that medical progress takes a disproportionate amount of resources to itself, an act unjustified because of the ultimate futility of all therapeutic efforts. Rather than continuing to try to advance therapeutic efforts, he calls for care for all in the face of illness—it sounds pleasant and unobjectionable, but the classical aim of medicine has been to cure, remedy, palliate, and heal and not just care.[15]

The vague emphasis given to care at the expense of other ends makes one wonder about its value. It is incomprehensible to call for abandonment of research, therapy, and treatment of the many conditions afflicting the elderly when we are much closer to therapeutic breakthroughs than ever before. Conquering new diseases is costly and difficult, but the only alternative is to accede to them, which both modern medicine and progressive culture have generally been unwilling to do.

In *Setting Limits* Callahan regarded death as a good for some, and he presented a very gloomy view of the lives of the elderly, debilitated, and handicapped. In *What Kind of Life* not only did Callahan see death as a good and life as an evil, but he presents curing, healing, and medical treatment as futile and ultimately evil in some circumstances. What has been the pride of so much of American society he sees as a painful and costly exercise in futility. At best, cures are only partial measures that cannot bring real relief, and all medical technologies are, as Willard Gaylin says, "half-way technologies" because everyone will die despite the best technological efforts.[16] This dour assessment is certainly questionable, for an appendectomy, for example, can save the life of a child for years—hardly a half-way technology or temporary fix.

Callahan calls for a health-care policy that strives for "compression of morbidity"—limiting the struggle against diseases entailing long-term morbidity before death.[17] Thus, treatments for cancer and arteriosclerosis should be halted if they would unduly delay death and increase morbidity. He claims that we are spending money to treat these conditions rather than buy health, which he sees as an invalid expenditure of scarce funds. But is not preserving the lives of these patients "buying health" in a looser but still legitimate sense?

In *What Kind of Life* Callahan denigrates the role of good health in life and demeans the part it can play in integral human fulfillment. His view makes the pursuit of health beyond the natural lifespan not merely optional, as it was in the traditional morality, but morally objectionable because it wastes precious resources.[18] Good health is not universally associated with happiness or serenity, and life lived with full health and vigor can be unhappy. Callahan calls the desire for health and wholeness a passion which he suggests should be resisted like lust, greed, and envy and should be replaced by a desire for altruism. Even though good health does not entail happiness, it is ordinarily a necessity for happiness. He rejects programs that would deny treatment to those who abuse their health because this would violate the ethical norms of medicine.[19] Denying the elderly care would be unjust, but would it be any less unjust than denying the elderly all forms of medical treatment?

Medical treatment can only forestall the effects of aging and decline, justification, he claims, for denying curative treatment to the elderly. But he fails to see that this also justifies denying medical treatments for the disabled. He fails to see the difference between cure and palliation, and while not all conditions can be definitively and completely cured, many can be palliated, enabling us to count them successes. Insulin treatments, for example, do not cure diabetes but do enable many to live full lives for many years. While this may not be an absolute cure, it would certainly be good enough for many whose only other option is death.

Callahan's distinction between curing and caring is really quite simplistic, for medicine aims at bringing conditions into remission, palliating or managing symptoms, and performing other types of actions to deal with diseases; it does not simply either "cure" or "care." One cannot lump all forms of therapeutic actions not included in patient maintenance under the category of "curing" and demand they be abandoned when a patient reaches a certain age.[20]

In urging the priority of care over cure, Callahan is taking the perspective of a healthy middle-aged man and not that of what the disabled community calls a TAB: temporarily able-bodied. Unlike the disabled who want cures and see them as more justified than care, he only wants to offer a care that often does little to help the sick or disabled. He characterizes the desire to continue living on the part of the elderly as obsessive. One can agree that we need not buy life at any cost, but his call to abandon all curative treatment for the elderly does not square with his vision of a wise and mature society in which there is fair and equal access to health care. This vision would seem to require that the elderly be given the same inexpensive treatment as is given the younger, particularly when it would be clinically efficacious.

Economic Pessimism

Callahan complains at the outset of *What Kind of Life* that the current crisis in health-care financing is so critical that no common solution would work effectively. Allowing the government or free market to function alone would not adequately solve the problem of overspending for health care.[21] He criticizes both the conservative and old liberal schemes for dealing with health-care expenses, and yet his proposal to radically reduce the level and kinds of care offered the aged, the sick, and the dying is ultimately rather traditional. His is a liberal solution, in which he joins a new contempt of the elderly with the traditional liberal call for massive government intervention. One has to doubt how novel and imaginative this proposal really is and wonder if others in the past have not considered but rejected it as practical but ruthless toward the elderly. His call for furthering socialized medicine is now somewhat anachronistic because it will probably not bring better medical care, but only lower medical expenditures.

Callahan is unidimensional in his thought, explicitly contending that economic concerns override all others. Allowing financial concerns to overcome all others is bad ethics and questionable social policy. It requires one of the world's most productive societies to voluntarily arrest its productivity, despite its long-standing tradition of progress and high demand for the fruits of this productivity because he considers the expenditures excessive.

He claims we spend significantly more on health care than other nations, despite the fact that our national health is not significantly better.[22] This is probably due to the fact that a great deal of this money is allocated to research and testing, which is ultimately for the benefit of other countries and significantly increases the costs of our own care and treatments. These higher expenditures also probably result from the rather high level of compensation we give physicians in this country. Other countries would not tolerate the drain that physicians impose on our health-care resources.

Because we have made such great progress in the past half century, we need a bias in favor of imposing limits on health care rather than of promoting progress and indulging individual desires, for we can now legitimately slow progress, or so Callahan claims.[23] We need to adopt a more "symmetrical" approach to health care in which expenditures for treatments have to show the power to enhance radically the quality of life in the short term to be justified.[24] But it is not just individual desires for cures that must be curbed, but the desires and aspirations of our entire society for more cures and therapies as well.

Callahan denies that advances in technology, greater efficiency, or freer market systems would reduce expenditures to an acceptable level.[25] He declares that cost-containment efforts have failed and will continue to fail to curb expenditures for health care.[26] As in *Setting Limits*, so also in *What Kind of Life*, he does not trust traditional market mechanisms to be able to limit expenditures, and he believes that allowing the market to operate freely would create a morally intolerable situation.[27]

Callahan claims that catastrophe would follow from total rejection of his proposal, and he denies it would be better to enact parts of his program incrementally than to reject it in toto.[28] He calls for national health insurance to provide adequate access to health care for those who cannot personally afford it, but he does not face the possibility that such a system could increase expenditures for health care. A national health insurance would also give individuals wider access to health care and limit the market forces that could effectively curb demand if allowed to operate more freely.

Setting Priorities in the Allocation of Health Care

The health-care system should provide the most benefits to the population as a whole, ensuring that all receive care, comfort, and support during illness.[29] Callahan does not envision medicine guaranteeing simple and readily available cures for the sick and elderly, and he emphasizes caring for and curing illnesses that result in premature death or thwart human aspirations.

In *What Kind of Life* Callahan claims it is necessary to devise a set of "reasonable aspirations" concerning care and treatment.[30] In essence, these aspirations are limited to avoiding death during the natural lifespan and meeting the cognitive, emotional, and functional needs of all who can profit from them.[31] From these "reasonable aspirations," a set of standards for providing care and a hierarchy of care and treatment can be established.

When it comes to technology assessment, the only standards Callahan permits are those of pure economic pragmatism, and he subordinates professional ideals and commitments to these concerns. Technology is wrongly developed and employed if it radically extends the life of the aged, or, in Callahan's words, if it threatens "societally necessary limits on the frontiers of aging and individual need." Effective but expensive technologies producing long-term social or ethical problems should be avoided.[32] These could be commendable principles, but they need specification and qualification to be fully permissible.

Callahan wants to raise the level of health of subgroups that fall below average with the exception of the elderly.[33] He proposes the principle of sufficiency to set priorities for rationing medical resources and to curb expenditures. The principle of sufficiency holds that society must determine an adequate level of health for other societal functions to be carried out.[34] Investments in medical research must meet his criteria of symmetry—to be morally permissible, a balance between saving life and maintaining a good quality of life must be sought. His principle is simplistic and naive, however, because often the treatments that appear most costly and least productive in the short run are the most beneficial in the long run. His principle should be replaced with one holding that good science and research should be pursued and bad science and medicine suppressed.

Callahan demands that our society weigh the cultural as well as the medical impact of medical success when evaluating proposals to fund medical research or employ medical resources.[35] And this impact should be examined not only cross-culturally but also in an adequate historical framework, as should his proposals for radically limiting research and development of medical technology and withholding care. Even further, not only should the impact of developing and advancing care be examined in the way he demands, but withdrawing care and medical treatment for the categories he mentions should be similarly examined. But there is a certain lack of symmetry in his requirement that the impact of technology be examined, for he only wants to scrutinize the impact of the provision of treatment and not their withdrawal on culture, medicine, and science. A truly symmetrical approach would examine the effects of both of these choices.

Callahan holds that we should aspire to a level of care that would be sufficient for us to function as a society.[36] But he does not say what sort of society we should be trying to sustain with the health care we seek. Different levels of social development require different levels of health, as the level of health required for a society of wandering sheepherders would be different from a society of technocrats. This standard for health care is too formal, vague, and empty to be a sufficient guide.

Rationing Health Care

Callahan advances his proposal by developing a doctrine of the common good, and he wants individuals to focus primarily on advancing the good of the group at the expense of the individual, which is the recipe for totalitarianism. He will not allow individual concerns for health to come into play, as the individual cannot be allowed to negate the principle that health is to be directed at achieving common goals.[37] Classical social philosophy gave much thought to this issue, and it affirmed that the common good of a community could not be properly advanced if the natural rights of individuals were not properly and legitimately protected. Classical moral thought would hold that all persons have a natural right to readily providable, inexpensive, and clinically effective medical treatments, irrespective of their age. Such a tradition would consider Callahan's claims invalid.[38] Callahan is not clear about the relationship of the individual to the group, and it seems as if he is calling for a simple and explicit subordination of the individual to the community.

To justify his rationing proposal, Callahan asks how much health a society as a whole needs. What he should be asking is what a society owes individuals and what individuals owe society in terms of consumption of health-care resources. There are some aspects of an individual life that can be legitimately subordinated to the good of the group, but not where serious moral injustice would result. One cannot advance the good of the whole so radically that one denies morally required curative measures to an individual or group.

Callahan insists that restraints be imposed on the general public's demand for health care. Rather than allowing the medical profession or the marketplace to impose these restraints, he would empower government and elected officials to do so.[39] He calls for publicly supported medicine and compares private medicine to private armies and fire brigades.[40] At the most basic level of providing care and treatment, the government should work to maintain a balance and should reduce age-group and socioeconomic gaps in the distribution of health-care resources and assure that no one would be deprived of basic health care that is available to the population as a whole.[41] But a more nuanced approach to this issue is required, for Callahan does not draw any distinctions about the various types of care to be withheld. The most basic difficulty, however, with this proposal, as Lawrence DeBrock pointed out, is that the most efficient mechanism for disciplining the appetite for medical care is the free market, not the government, because the latter is primarily a political rather than an economic institution. Callahan will not give the market free rein because of the "moral jeopardy" involved in so doing. We claim there is greater moral jeopardy in his totalitarian proposal than there would be in giving market mechanisms greater latitude.

Callahan naively believes the government, which has been accustomed to liberally spending for medical care for decades, would be able to resist strong political pressures to not just continue these policies but expand them as the population grows older.[42] He sees the government as the best agency for reducing expenditures, and yet this same government has been one of the primary agents for increasing them in the past. He wants legislators to cut back on health-care expenditures, and yet he admits that Medicare and Medicaid have been quite resistant to cutbacks.[43]

His belief that politicians would be able to stand up against the tide of elders demanding more and more health care is incredible, for there is no historical precedent for such political independence.[44] In recent months we have seen repeated instances where elected officials and government agencies have not had the political wherewithal to withstand the political pressures that demand for health care can impose; only the free market can offer the sort of resistance necessary to curb medical expenditures.

Callahan seems to discount the intensity of the opposition the elderly would present to his proposal. It is quite unlikely that the elderly would accept the reduced care he is demanding for them and more likely that they would continue to press hard for the level of medical treatments they are now paying, particularly after having paid for Medicare and Medicaid for years. There is some justification for their claims, and they would consider it a grave injustice to be as radically deprived of medical treatment as they would be in their final years under his regime.

In *What Kind of Life* Callahan abandoned his demand that private funds not be allowed to be used for health care, even though this would destroy the equitable features of the system he proposed in *Setting Limits* and even though it would not put any curbs on private spending.[45] The government should be responsible for providing basic levels of medical care and treatment, but employee benefit programs should provide care at the second tier, and the market would be allowed to flourish at the third tier, which would include the most expensive, novel, and least effective forms of care.

The poor and unemployed would suffer relatively greater burdens under this system than they would under that proposed in *Setting Limits* and they would be denied the benefits accorded not only to the wealthy but also to workers as well.[46] In *What Kind of Life* Callahan wants government to assume the burden of rationing and appears willing to try a mixed system of government control and market mechanisms, even though he believes it probably would not work. He discusses who should make decisions about rationing health care, which he did not do in *Setting Limits*. He believes there should be public discussions of rationing health-care resources, and he claims that decisions should ultimately be made by legislative processes.[47] But there is still no mention of those who object to limitations on the basis of conscience. The public must take part in sustained discussions, but after the discussions are over, bureaucratic agencies must make and enforce the decisions.

Callahan argues against making rationing decisions for individuals in such a way that physicians would have to inform patients that they would be denied care because this would put the doctor in an untenable position.[48] Physicians should have a central role in setting standards for rationing care and treatment, but they should not have the onerous task of having to refuse to care for patients. Callahan, however, does not face the question of who would make these decisions. Who would want this thankless job that demands all of the qualities of an Uncle Scrooge and a hangman? By exempting physicians from this task, Callahan is implicitly admitting that his proposal for rationing health care is a dirty business, one that no reputable physician would want to be associated with. What he fails to see is that it is such an abhorrent undertaking that no one else would want it either—that its victims would primarily be the elderly only increases the task's repugnance.

There are a number of problems that Callahan does not confront in *What Kind of Life*. He gives lip service to claims that individual rights should be protected but does not explicitly permit individuals to dissent from his system, and one senses that he would impose his rationing system against popular wishes if he deemed it necessary and could find a way to do so. He assumes that legislatures would welcome and endorse his proposals, but if they did not provide what he wants, would he resort to the coercion and totalitarianism of *Setting Limits?* And what if voters would want physicians to make rationing decisions on a case-by-case basis? What if legislation would curb physician fees and require curative treatments for the elderly to limit expenditures and give fairer treatment for the elderly? What if legislation would increase desire for health care rather than curb it? It is quite likely that many would not support his harsh and trying proposals, and one suspects that he would urge straightforwardly imposing his criteria without the consent of a community. He would only accept legislation that would protect physicians legally and not make them responsible for rationing decisions.

Conclusion

If *What Kind of Life* was meant to clarify and strengthen the proposals for age-based rationing of *Setting Limits,* it has failed, for it reveals many of the previously hidden faults of age-based rationing. *Setting Limits* sought to argue that age-based rationing was both just and cost effective, but it showed itself to be a failure. *What Kind of Life* is broader in scope and no more competent than *Setting Limits,* and its demands for fuller governmental involvement in rationing schemes only enhances the totalitarian character of Callahan's scheme. In *Setting Limits,* Callahan's totalitarianism was implicit and hidden, but in *What Kind of Life* it has become explicit and overt. Callahan seeks a program that would provide scarce medical resources to our complex and pluralistic society with fairness, justice, compassion, and equity, but he is blind to the unjust burdens his age-based rationing scheme inflicts on the elderly. To solve the daunting problem of providing for the valid health-care needs of our society, a more nuanced and sophisticated approach than Callahan's age-based rationing scheme is needed. His proposal unduly burdens the elderly, undermines our democratic freedoms, and would not guarantee any significant reductions in expenditures. Rationing scarce medical resources is a complex and difficult problem that will take its toll on us, but it is to be hoped that it will not demand the price Callahan's age-based rationing proposal does.

NOTES

1. Daniel Callahan, *What Kind of Life: The Limits of Medical Progress* (New York: Simon and Schuster, 1990), 34, 153, 30. Callahan seems to be guilty of unrelieved pessimism, for he is apparently only able to see the harm and not the benefit of medical care and treatment. His current proposal is a recipe for abandoning pursuit of a great part of the most interesting and beneficial research now being conducted in many areas. He blames much of the current overuse of health care on

the World Health Organization's definition of health. But how many people even know of this definition, which was issued forty-three years ago by an organization that has little impact on the daily lives of the vast majority of Americans? He believes that demand for high-cost curative medical treatment must be curbed and that the government, not the marketplace, is the best institution to accomplish this, but it has been the government that has fostered demand by its programs. Callahan fears the moral hazard of not allowing the poor and needy to have access to medical care and treatment, but he does not fear the moral hazard of denying the elderly simple and effective curative medical treatments.

2. Ibid., 149–51.

3. Callahan tries to recapture the term "care" from the pro-lifers who have argued for years that care (meaning food and water, protection from exposure, and sanitary care) should be given to all because denial of these culpably kills by omission. He agrees that these should be given, but then claims that one can withhold everything else without culpability from the elderly. This view lacks symmetry.

4. Ibid., 202. "By a categorical standard I mean, in contrast, the use of some relatively objective, required public standard for the provision of particular forms of health care, or for the cessation or limitation of care. Examples would be the use of age as a limit on some forms of treatment for the elderly (and the main way of restricting that frontier), and the use of firm outcome or other efficacy standards for other patients (as the main way of restricting the frontier of individual curative needs)."

5. Ibid., 66–67, 197–98, 117. This comparison with schools is useful, for, freed from government regulation, American private and religious schools have generally provided superior education at a lower cost than have American public schools.

6. Ibid., 180.

7. Ibid., 177.

8. Ibid., 164–66. This principle would apply to all but the elderly. If, for example, a healthy eighty-year-old required a curative treatment that would probably provide another ten years of active life, it would be denied, though such a treatment would probably be given to a sixty-five-year-old individual.

9. Ibid. In *Setting Limits* Callahan refused to consider the demographic solution to the problem of controlling medical costs: increasing the size of the younger population. And in *What Kind of Life* he still refuses to consider it, and he speaks only of finding new ways of cutting costs, not of raising new revenues or finding new ways to support the elderly and infirm.

10. Ibid., 165. Callahan believes this standard would only restrict the provision of medical treatments for the elderly, but in practice it could also severely prohibit the provision of much treatment for the disabled and handicapped as well. This reveals another totalitarian trait of his work: his willingness to subordinate urgent immediate personal goods for long-term, less-than-urgent social goods.

11. Ibid., 191.

12. Ibid., 156, 176–77. In Callahan's model, curative treatments are only found at level three and above, and the elderly would be generally denied these levels of treatment.

13. Ibid., 202.

14. One suspects from this that Callahan's real concern in *Setting Limits* is not so much promoting intergenerational equity as reducing expenditures. One hears nothing, for instance, of an obligation to advance research for future generations.

15. Ibid., 187–88.

16. Ibid., 48–50, 100, 101 (Gaylin quote).

17. Ibid., 174. This strategy is directed most precisely at the elderly and less specifically at others.

18. Callahan says that our nation should follow the lead of good armies and not advance beyond our supply lines, but often the best armies forage for their supplies and fight to take those of the enemy. All good armies function and perform despite what they consider to be critical shortages. He fails to see that it is the common opinion of military commanders that the truly great leaders were bold enough to do precisely that. Such boldness often inspires armies to greater efforts than would otherwise be expected.

19. Ibid., 210, 39. But would not categorical denials of beneficial and low-cost care to the elderly who could derive significant benefits from it equally violate that ethic? What Callahan would not even consider permitting for the young, he feels is a necessity with the elderly.

20. Ibid. He also draws a distinction between "care" and "minimal levels of care" and asserts that a decent health-care system should seek to provide minimal levels of care for all. Does this mean that some forms of care, as he defines it, are to be denied even the young?

21. Ibid., 20–21. Callahan wants to reduce the outlay for health care resources but does not want the market mechanisms, which usually perform this function, to operate freely to accomplish this goal. His justification for this view is the assertion that they have not operated effectively in the past and they should not be given a second chance. If they have not operated as he thinks they should, it is probably because of a number of factors have intervened to prevent their effective functioning. He fails to see that medicine is the last remnant of the medieval guild system and that attempts to regulate or support it by government control will only perpetuate its inefficiency. Opening health care resource allocation more fully to free market mechanisms will not create the moral dangers he fears because of well-established legal and professional safeguards. And the moral dangers he fears could not be much worse than those that would be created under his regime. Government regulation of health care could radically inhibit recruitment of health care workers because it could not meet the financial demands these workers would impose. Biomedical research and health care practice are profoundly demanding, and large financial incentives are often needed to attract qualified people.

22. Ibid., 18–19, 117. While acknowledging that we have a lower quality of health per dollar spent in relation to other advanced countries, Callahan is calling for even lower expenditures for health. Should he not be calling for more efficient use of the dollars we spend? Would Americans tolerate even poorer health, given the fact that they are now paying so much for the low quality of health care they are

already getting for their dollar? And if we adopt his standards for providing health care and give no curative treatments to the elderly, our level of health will fall significantly below that of other advanced nations. Does he expect the American people to accept that? What is lacking in his study is an investigation of why we suffer poorer health, despite higher expenditures than other countries. He refuses to admit it, but improving efficiency seems to be morally and economically imperative.

23. Ibid., 115. Civil libertarians should be concerned with this proposal as it would imply giving the state extraordinary powers to intervene in private choices about levels of medical treatment to be given. Callahan claims that health is primarily a social good, but it is most strictly a private good that has immediate and direct social implications. To account for our individual and societal obligations toward health, both aspects of health must be given adequate consideration.

24. Ibid., 166. We are the technological and scientific society par excellence, and Callahan's call for us to curb our desire for health care because of economic factors would strike at the root and heart of our culture and society. He complains that American technology is waning, but if the restraints imposed by his demands for symmetrical health care are observed, technological research would be stifled even further, for scientists and researchers would not be free to pursue what they see as the most promising avenues of research.

25. Ibid., ch. 3.

26. Ibid., 260. But rather than failing, maybe we have created the most efficient health-care system possible, given its technological capability, wealth, and understanding of the moral commitments of medicine and society. And if that is the case, it is quite unlikely that use of political or legislative mechanisms would bring about further reductions in expenditures. The most effective mechanism might well be to eliminate government involvement in health care, thereby allowing prices to move to levels tolerable by society.

27. Ibid., 21. An uncontrolled free market of medical treatment would destroy any balance in the allocation of health care, for the wealthy could obtain far more than the poor. We would have to ask, however, whether the moral climate of compulsory denial of medical treatment of the elderly is any less objectionable than the moral peril that would result from diminishing government involvement in health care.

28. Ibid., 214.

29. Ibid., 187–88.

30. Callahan does not mention, however, that virtually everyone believes his aspirations for health care are reasonable or necessary and not excessive or irrational. Even the maddest among us believe ourselves to be cogent, rational, and intelligent.

31. Ibid., 197–98, 67–68. For Callahan, meeting bodily needs for cures during the natural lifespan is a legitimate aspiration, but this becomes a hopeless and unworkable dream for those who are older. Why this is so hopeless and impractical is not entirely clear.

32. Ibid., 167, 165. Here we see Callahan's pessimism again, for he displays a remarkable lack of confidence in our society to reach a consensus about difficult social issues or ethicists to resolve complex social and moral issues.

33. Ibid., 130. It is quite permissible for them to have a level of health far below the average simply because they are elderly, and again this does not comport with his vision of a wise and mature society.

34. Ibid., 127. One wonders why he does not claim that we could reasonably aspire to a level of health equal to that of other advanced nations. Given that we are richer and have more means available than do many other nations, why would not such an aspiration be reasonable? And if it would be, why would not the current levels of expenditures be reasonable and sufficient?

35. Ibid., 169–71. This is a valuable insight, but it should be applied more broadly.

36. Ibid., 138–42.

37. Ibid., 191.

38. See Joseph Boyle, "The Concept of Health and the Right to Health Care," *Social Thought* 3 (Summer 1977): 5–17.

39. Callahan, *What Kind of Life,* 206–9. He envisions the government, through HCFA (the Health Care Financing Administration), regulating medical expenditures. Yet the government would be a weak instrument for controlling costs as this agency will be more responsive to political pressure to provide care and treatment than it will be to pressure such as Callahan would impose.

40. Ibid., 194.

41. Ibid., 198.

42. Ibid., 212–14. It is peculiar that he now would call on government to force reductions in expenditures because (as he admits) government involvement in health care after World War II played a large part in creating the present troubles by giving such relatively free access to medical care.

43. Ibid., 199, 118.

44. If Callahan wants institutions other than the marketplace to curb demand for health care, he should enlist the churches in his efforts, for they have more influence than do politicians, but they probably have too many moral objections to his proposal to give it the solid support it needs to succeed.

45. Ibid., 191.

46. Everything Callahan found wrong in our health-care system in *Setting Limits,* he seems to be espousing in his *What Kind of Life,* for in *Setting Limits* he argued vigorously against allowing any social or economic class greater access to health care than any other. But in *What Kind of Life* he claims that such unequal access is truly fair, just and equitable. Will the real Daniel Callahan, please, stand up?

47. Ibid., 206–7. But one can wonder what kind of discussion it would be when individuals such as Callahan are saying that everything but the categorical limits he espouses would fail?

48. Ibid., 208.

Notes on Contributors

HADLEY V. ARKES is the Edward Ney Professor of Jurisprudence and American Institutions at Amherst College. He is the author of *The Marshall Plan and the National Interest, The Philosopher in the City, First Things,* and *Beyond the Constitution.*

ROBERT L. BARRY, O.P., is a visiting assistant professor of religious studies at the University of Illinois at Urbana-Champaign. He is the author of *Medical Ethics* and *The Distant Edge of Life,* as well as numerous articles.

GERARD V. BRADLEY is a professor of law at the University of Illinois at Urbana-Champaign. His publications include *Church-State Relationships Today;* "Slaying the Dragon of Politics with the Sword of Law," *Illinois Law Review;* "Dogmatomacy: A 'Privatization' Theory of the Religion Clause Cases," *St. Louis University Law Review;* and "Imagining the Past and Remembering the Future: The Supreme Court's History of the Establishment Clause," *Connecticut Law Review.*

LAWRENCE DeBROCK is an associate professor of economics at the University of Illinois at Urbana-Champaign. His publications include "Market Structure, Innovation and Optimal Patient Care," *Journal of Law and Economics;* "The Effects of Provider Control of Blue Shield Plans on Health Care Markets," *Economic Inquiry;* "Do HMO's Produce Specific Services More Efficiently?," *Economic Inquiry;* and "Competition and Market Failure in the Hospital Industry: A Review of the Evidence," *Medical Care Review.*

ROBERT A. DESTRO is an associate professor of law, Columbus School of Law, Catholic University of America. His publications include "Equality, Social Welfare and Equal Protection," *Harvard Journal of Law and Public Policy;* "Abortion and the Constitution: The Need for a Life-Protective Amendment," *California Law Review;* and "Quality of Life Ethics and Constitutional Jurisprudence: The Demise of Natural Rights and Equal Protection for the Disabled and Incompetent," *Journal of Contemporary Health Law & Policy.*

ROBERT P. GEORGE is an assistant professor in the Department of Politics, Princeton University, and a member of the New Jersey and Pennsylvania bars. His publications include "Human Flourishing as a Criterion of Morality: A Critique of Perry's Naturalism," *Tulane Law Review;* and "Recent Criticism of Natural Law Theory," *University of Chicago Law Review.*

MARSHALL KAPP is a professor of legal medicine and the course director, Department of Medicine in Society, Wright State University School of Medicine. His publications include "Health Care Tradeoffs Based on Age: Ethically Confronting the 'R' Word," *The Pharos of Alpha Omega Alpha;* "Response to the Living Will Furor: Directives for Maximum Care," *American Journal of Medicine;* "Enforcing Patient Preferences: Linking Payment for Medical Care to Informed Consent," *Journal of the American Medical Association;* Health Care Delivery and the Elderly: Teaching Old Patients New Tricks," *Cumberland Law Review;* and "Legal and Ethical Implications of Health Care Reimbursement by Diagnosis Related Groups," *Law, Medicine & Health Care.*